GAME OVER
OR
GAME ON?

GAME OVER
OR
GAME ON?

HOW PRO ATHLETES LEAVE SPORTS AND ENJOY THE GAME OF LIFE

DAVID OSTROWSKY

mill city press, minneapolis mn

Copyright © 2014 by David Ostrowsky

Mill City Press, Inc.
322 First Avenue N, 5th floor
Minneapolis, MN 55401
612.455.2293
www.millcitypublishing.com

ISBN-13: 978-1-62652-622-8
LCCN: 2014900035

Printed in the United States of America

To My Wife Lauren,

Who Makes Life a Fun Game

~CONTENTS~

CHAPTER I

Where Are They Now?

Sports Illustrated subscribers come back from their July 4th vacations and know that buried in the avalanche of mail is the 'Where Are They Now?' issue. Dubbed a double issue, 'Where Are They Now?' is the thickest and arguably one of the most fascinating issues of the year. Generations of sports fans learn how their childhood heroes are currently spending their time. As readers sit in their dentist waiting rooms or lounge on their back porches, they breeze through the image laden pages. The issue serves as an endless succession of happy-go-lucky stories--even about athletes whom many of us have perceived as underachievers, braggarts, and even villains. Lawrence Taylor? "Saved By Golf." Bo Jackson? "Bo Knows Cooking." If a story makes it into the light hearted pages of 'Where Are They Now?' it is of the feel good variety. The issue is the happy answer to the unfortunate tales depicting broke, injured, and miserable athletes that buzz through airwaves and webpages on a seemingly weekly basis.

The following pages are similar to 'Where Are They Now?' in the sense that they provide a glimpse into the current successes enjoyed by various former professional athletes. Some were superstars, others borderline professionals. Some are multi-millionaires while others still have to work into their mid-eighties to pay the bills. The tie that binds them is their ability to realize that life doesn't end when sports does. They understand that their timespans as professional athletes represent a very small fraction of their natural lifespans. For the purposes of this book, the athletes quoted, profiled, and analyzed are enjoying their "retirement periods."

The magical carpet ride of childhood dreams turning into reality has an expiration date. It may come to a screeching halt or wither away slowly, but it does end well before the half time of one's life. Even for the most highly tenured pro athletes, careers come to a close somewhere in the second quarter, probably before the two minute warning. If the average athlete retires in his or her early thirties and the average human life spans nearly 80 years, then it seems that there is still a lot of living to do after exiting the world of professional athletics.

Hopefully, the ensuing stories do not merely summarize the details regarding where former athletes are now, but how and why they got there. Along the way, their decisions and lifestyle alterations paved the way for a graceful retirement period, at least in relation to many of their contemporaries. Their paths in retirement have all diverged from a common starting point: success in the public arena at a ridiculously young age. One would think it would be a perfect recipe for happiness. For countless Americans currently toiling in dead end jobs and navigating through a treacherous financial landscape, the prospect of retiring before turning 40 would seem like nirvana. Yet sadly, and sometimes tragically, not all pro athletes have enjoyed such a graceful retirement period.

From the perspective of many fans, the idea of athletes struggling in retirement seems like the ultimate paradox. Being a professional athlete is one of the most enviable careers. Everyone dreams about it, but then it ends so young, and what comes after? Amateur athletes at the high school and collegiate levels are encouraged to have a backup plan in the event that their professional athletic careers don't materialize. But what about having a backup plan for those whose dreams do materialize? In most careers, people reach their professional apex during the middle-aged years while athletes often do so before their 30th birthday. Even the overwhelming majority of athletes who manage to stay relatively healthy retire before their 40th birthday.

Unsurprisingly, a Google search of "former pro athletes where are they now" predominantly displays results that are nothing short of depressing. Keywords that frequently arise are "financial trouble." Even though modern athletes have lucrative contracts and can sustain lengthier careers with ample time for offseason training, they are nonetheless susceptible to hard times. Dragged into poor investments, stalked by freeloaders, and saddled with medical problems, many pro athletes get shocked by harsh economic jolts when robust paychecks are no longer flowing into their bank accounts. In 2009, *Sports Illustrated* issued a report stating that within five years of retirement, an estimated 60 % of former NBA players are broke. Ironically, when compared to other professional athletes, NBA players reap the most robust financial rewards. The mindboggling report articulated a disturbingly true message: athletes of all generations are susceptible to the sometimes tumultuous rollercoaster that is life.

Former Boston Celtics great Antoine Walker is the epitome of such a precipitous downfall. In 2012 *Sports Illustrated* published a story titled "If Antoine Walker Shimmies, But It's In Boise, Is He Really Shimmying?" The story chronicled how Walker, a former NBA veteran who earned over $100 million, had to declare bankruptcy after leaving the NBA. The usual culprits accounted for Walker's demise: a lavish lifestyle, poor investments, severe gambling losses, and bankrolling dozens of friends and relatives for fancy cars, jewelry, etc. At the time of the article, Walker was playing for the Idaho Stampede of the NBA Development League, making less than $25,000 per year. He shared a two bedroom apartment that went for $915 per month in rent. He couldn't afford to own a car and lived off microwaveable food.

Walker's story is a fairy tale when it is juxtaposed to the plight of boxing legend Joe Louis. The son of a sharecropper, Louis rose up through the ranks of amateur and professional boxing to become the world heavyweight champion, a title he owned from 1937 to 1949. When he left the ring, a cocaine addiction and bouts with mental illness left him destitute and downright dysfunctional. The Caesar's Palace Casino in Las Vegas hired him as a greeter, a job which involved signing autographs, shaking customers' hands, betting with house money when the action seemed a little slow and playing golf with special guests. Louis lived and worked at Caesar's Palace until he died of a massive heart attack in 1981.

Stories of financial trouble are not necessarily due to athletes blowing millions of dollars on risky ventures. They can also stem from those who never had millions of dollars because they played in an age when athletes had to work side jobs and think about preparing themselves for later endeavors in life. There once was a time when even some of the most accomplished ones made fairly modest earnings. For most of the 20th century, athletes lived amongst the general populace. The majority didn't have the financial means to live in gated communities and drive cars with tinted windows. They were not living in a different stratosphere from the rest of civilization. They had to leave a modest paying career (athletics) and learn an entirely novel skill set in order to adapt to a new career.

Don Larsen is the only pitcher to have ever thrown a perfect game in the World Series. In 2012, he had to auction off the jersey he donned when scripting athletic history. It was for the most noble of causes: to help fund his granddaughter's college education. The jersey earned him $756,000 in the open market, more than quadrupling his aggregate career earnings. Larsen made a living playing baseball, so perhaps he shouldn't be considered an embodiment of working class struggles. But he does exemplify the predicament of earlier ballplayers. Even the biggest stars of Larsen's generation such as Joe DiMaggio and Mickey Mantle relied on autograph sessions for income at the end of their lives. It was more than a public appearance; it was a way to continue earning a living.

The downfalls of formerly prosperous individuals serve as cautionary tales for how a surplus of money and time may be more of a toxic combination than a best of both worlds scenario. In a sense, it is eerily similar to winning the lottery and not having to work another day. Many go flat-out broke. In another sense, the story of professional athletes' profligacy and recklessness is an allegorical tale of America's recent financial struggles. It is just that pro athletes, more so than any other sector of the population, have the capability to waste so much money.

By no means do the following stories encapsulate every former athlete currently making the most out of his or her "retirement." Rather what ensues is a potpourri of tales chronicling how athletes can become politicians, actors, lawyers, businessmen, broadcasters, community activists, coaches, and educators. After devoting tens of thousands of hours towards mastering a specific skill, many athletes realize that retirement from sports is an optimal time to learn a new craft or pursue other interests.

In a broader sense, retirement from professional sports can be viewed through a double prism. It can be viewed as the great neutralizer, bringing larger than life athletes back down to the level of mere mortals. Signing autographs for sycophantic fans gives way to running errands. Picking up the kids from kindergarten and shopping at the aisles of Whole Foods supplant batting practice and morning skates. Boredom, despondency, and loneliness can surface when there is no longer the stimulation of playing in sold-out arenas and being surrounded by dozens of teammates, coaches, reporters, and fans on a daily basis.

On the other hand, retirement from athletics can serve as a head start for pursuing other enviable careers. And nowhere does that phenomenon manifest itself more strongly than in the arena of broadcasting. The majority of people seeking to become on air broadcasters in a hot market such as Boston, New York or Los Angeles often spend years toiling in internships and low-paying assistant jobs in remote outposts for something that may never materialize. Those who were blessed with the talent to reach the holy grail of professional sports have every right to get a "head start" in pursuing the cushy profession of broadcasting. No one cashes in on the cache of pro athleticism more so than some national broadcasters such as Tom Jackson and Trent Dilfer. Analyzing the nation's most popular game on the world's most popular sports network (ESPN) equates to earning millions of dollars. They were respectable football players who have become national icons in the sports broadcasting world. The networks need the expertise and cache of former pro athletes and are especially willing to pay top dollar to those who can provide charisma. Name recognition breeds strong ratings and ultimately happy executives. National sports broadcasters don't have to be former stars but they need to fall under the broad category of "marketable." It does say something about American culture that many athletes turned broadcasters are cementing their legacies by observing sports rather than playing them. Being able to smile in front of the camera and make the occasional controversial comment are invaluable assets. As long as the given individual has crossed the Fort Knox boundary of becoming a pro athlete, he or she is a potential candidate for becoming a mega superstar broadcaster.

The other obvious avenue for taking advantage of the proverbial head start is via coaching. Athletes, particularly those who had lengthy and successful careers, are often (but certainly not always) first in line for the coaching vacancies for their respective organizations. There is a level of comfort and trust. Similar to broadcasting, coaching allows one to stay in the game and remain affiliated with a former team. At least for the head coaches and managers, the salaries continue to be quite lucrative and in many cases, transcend those of the actual players.

However, many of the following pages illustrate ways that former great athletes have prospered in avenues outside of the broadcasting and coaching professions. Many other athletic and non-athletic opportunities abound. Often unfairly viewed as one-dimensional jocks, ex-pro athletes have also made creative, intellectual, and artistic contributions to society. There is no one category in which they can be associated with but the ensuing chapters detail several viable ones.

CHAPTER 2

Business: How the Rich Get Richer

(Or Try to Stay Rich)

Michael Jordan and Magic Johnson are living proof of how America gives a lucky few the means to ascend from rags to riches. Magic, originally born Earvin Johnson, was one of 10 siblings under the care of two blue collar workers who toiled tirelessly to make ends meet. Growing up in Lansing, Michigan, Johnson learned the game of basketball while his mother served as a school custodian and his dad manned a General Motors plant in town. Now Magic, CEO of Magic Johnson Enterprises and partial owner of the Los Angeles Dodgers, is one of California's most powerful businessmen.

Similar to Magic and many NBA players, Jordan was raised by a family with limited means. While he came from a two parent household in which bills were paid on time and food was put on the table, his background was a humble one: his grandfather was a sharecropper, his father an equipment supervisor.

Irrespective of lavish spending habits, Johnson and Jordan would have retired with exorbitant amounts of money had they never decided to pursue business ventures when they were done with hoops. But they have gone into business and have gotten a lot richer.

Jordan leveraged his globally famous brand name to launch an incredibly popular restaurant chain (Michael Jordan's Steakhouse) and has become an owner of the Charlotte Bobcats. Magic has emerged as one of the most influential people in the entire state of California. Magic and Michael of course represent the extreme case of former mega superstars parlaying their resources towards earning hundreds of millions of dollars in the business world. Even non-superstars in the modern age, particularly those who have enjoyed sustainable careers, have great financial resources to leverage towards business success. It wasn't always like that but it sure is now. There are no indisputable landmark dates when pro athletes went from earning respectable to otherworldly salaries. There were individuals such as Marvin Miller and Curt Flood whose audacious efforts allowed modern players to become free agents and be treated more like royalty than chattel. But for the purposes of this discussion, the development of the professional athlete's bloated contract can be perceived through a few arbitrary snapshots of history.

In 1930, during the onset of the Great Depression, Babe Ruth was asked to comment on how his $80,000 yearly salary eclipsed President Herbert Hoover's income of $75,000. He made the succinct remark that "I had a better year than the president." That season, Ruth posted a .359 batting average, 49 home runs, and 153 RBI while establishing himself as the premier slugger of his generation. Meanwhile Hoover's laissez-faire policies were something less than a smash hit.

On November 29, 1976, the New York Yankees signed Reggie Jackson to a five-year contract worth $2.96 million. Jackson hit .286 with 32 home runs and 110 RBI in his first season in the Bronx. Then there was Barry Bonds signing his $43.75 million contract with the San Francisco Giants during the winter meetings held in December 1992. Now athletes were making multi-million dollar yearly salaries.

The stars, long tenured veterans, and fringe players of the past century all paved the way for the current crop of athletes to become nearly instantaneous millionaires upon inking their first professional contract. By law, a professional athlete doesn't have to be Babe Ruth to earn the salary that the president makes. As of 2013, an NFL player cannot make less than $405,000 per year as long as he is on the roster for a specified number of days. The minimum wages for MLB, NBA, and

NHL players are $480,000, $473,604, and $525,000 respectively. The different player unions leave no stone unturned. For each sport, the collective bargaining agreement stipulates that salaries must increase by a certain increment on an annual basis to account for inflation.

Not everyone who donned a pro team's uniform can become a billionaire by embarking on a business career but many find self-fulfillment and enjoyment through parlaying their accumulated resources and wealth of free time towards personalized business ventures. There are dozens if not hundreds of tales of former athletes working in the business world to pursue a creative passion, interact with the public, seek intellectual stimulation, or merely pay the bills. The following pages chronicle some of the more fascinating ones.

A Tale of Two Real Estate Men

Magic Johnson and Dolph Schayes are both former Hall of Fame guards who come from working class backgrounds. When *Sports Illustrated* unveiled its list of the all-time Top 50 NBA Players to celebrate the league's 50 year anniversary, both made the list. And in retirement, both have spent more than a considerable amount of time working in the field of commercial real estate. But that's about where the comparisons end.

Schayes, one of basketball's all-time greatest shooters who starred for the Syracuse Nationals, runs a housing complex, East Ridge Apartments, in the Greater Syracuse area. Schayes' business partner is his son Danny, a good NBA pro in his own right, who enjoyed a solid career for the Denver Nuggets and Milwaukee Bucks among other franchises. At East Ridge, there is one receptionist but tenants typically interact with Dolph directly when issues arise. They sign a lease in his presence and personally shake his hand afterwards. There is no personal assistant to Mr. Schayes. At 85-years-old, he still has to be accountable for clogged toilets.

Many elderly Americans living in the Northeast Corridor, Hall of Fame athletes or not, naturally flock to Palm Beach or Palm Springs come Halloween time. Not for Schayes. Syracuse is still very much Schayes' domain as it comprises his professional, personal, and recreational world. For Schayes, his business is not just a means for making a living but also a way to stay attached to a community that is near and dear to his heart. Through his real estate business, Schayes has been able to maintain strong ties to the Syracuse community, particularly with older residents who still fondly remember his impeccable free throw shooting. To this day, he still runs into folks he has known for decades at town diners and coffee shops.

"I felt a real estate career would be lucrative. I enjoy doing it because I get to be creative. I like building things and I'm grateful for the fact that I have a career," explained the 12-time NBA All-Star who once played against the Boston Celtics in a four overtime game in 1953.

"Commercial real estate's been fine. It has its ups and downs. In the long run, it's been a good investment. It keeps me out of trouble. I like Syracuse, it's where all my family is but the winters are tough."

As far as retirement from athletics goes, Schayes has a broader and more timeworn perspective than most former pro athletes. It has been half a century since Dolph has been paid to play basketball. When the standout stopped playing, he made a seamless transition to coaching. One of his pupils was Wilt Chamberlain.

"You've got to do things with life. Real estate gives me freedom, helps pay the bills. It has been a good choice on my part."

Many former pro jocks have tried their hand at real estate. As Schayes has weathered the valleys and enjoyed the boom times of the real estate industry, he can look back and feel content that he chose the right non-basketball career in the later years of his life.

"I presume so many former pro athletes go into real estate because they want to make money. Money depends on locations, way you attack your situation, goals. Real estate is as good as an investment for ex-athletes as anything else. Some have done well, others not so well."

Diagonally across North America, Magic Johnson has done very, very well with real estate. Through accident of birth, Magic emerged as a superstar during the right time. As an all-world point guard for the Showtime Los Angeles Lakers in the 1980's, Magic socialized with such entertainment kingpins as Jack Nicholson, Bill Murray, and Michael Jackson. He was already forging partnerships with Hollywood luminaries and California business tycoons as a means of creating an unparalleled networking and personal branding bonanza. During Schayes' halcyon days as a star NBA guard, the hybrid athlete/entertainer was still in its embryonic stage. Schayes was a phenomenal player but not a bona fide celebrity.

With multiple exorbitant contracts and a dizzying number of endorsements, Magic left the game of basketball for good in 1996 after earning tens of millions of dollars. Real estate has helped him earn hundreds of millions. Basketball gave him the head start in business but no one could have predicted this kind of astronomical success. What makes Magic Johnson such a unique example is that so many mega rich athletes do fail in the business world, particularly in commercial real estate. Being named to All-Star teams and awarded MVP trophies can leave some with the feeling that the world is theirs to conquer, even if it is a business world completely foreign to them. That hasn't been the case with Johnson, a man everyone thought was supposed to have died years ago from the HIV virus. Magic's keen business acumen and megawatt personality have been a great one-two punch for wheeling and dealing commercial properties in Southern California.

Johnson, who likes to be addressed as Earvin in the business world, has become a globally recognized business leader with his commercial real estate holdings, partial ownership of the Dodgers, and portfolio of other assets. With his trademark half-moon smile, Magic Johnson is a match made in heaven for the sun splashed streets of Los Angeles.

"You have an individual who is very sincere, very authentic, who people in the city of Los Angeles trust. He is an extraordinary businessman who has done a great job of executing his strategies," said Ken Lombard, former president of the Johnson Development Corp. and a key mentor to Johnson in his transition from basketball to business. Meanwhile *LA Times* writer Roger Vincent referred to Magic's post-retirement period as one of the most successful post-game careers of any professional athlete.

It is not just that he has made an ungodly amount of money. The former Los Angeles Lakers guard has carved out a role as a liaison between big-money investors and the residents of urban neighborhoods who might become their customers in a variety of businesses including theaters, restaurants, stores, and apartment complexes. Magic has also done a lot of exemplary charitable work in the city that still idolizes him. He has leveraged his immense financial resources towards bankrolling real estate developments in dilapidated L.A. neighborhoods while also establishing the Magic Johnson Foundation, which promotes awareness of HIV and AIDS.

Similar to how he was as a player, Magic defies being pigeonholed into one category during his midlife years. He is a business magnate, real estate developer, philanthropist, broadcaster, team owner, spokesperson, and community activist. And in the cutthroat world of commercial real estate, he is blowing away the competition, just as he did as a player.

Wining and Dining

When one is in the midst of playing a sport for a living, there is little time to explore other interests. So retiring wealthy and early can be the perfect springboard for pursuing a non-sports related passion.

In the upper left hand quadrant of America, two former athletic legends, Tom Seaver and Shawn Kemp, have carved out their niche in the winery and dining industries respectively. Unlike many celebrity athletes who manage their enterprises from afar, the erstwhile ace pitcher and ferocious power forward are very much a part of the day-to-day fabrication of their businesses.

Towards the latter end of Seaver's Hall of Fame career, his brother-in-law asked him the straightforward but open-ended question of what he was going to do upon retiring from baseball. Without hesitation, Seaver, a lifelong wine connoisseur, answered, "I'm going back to California to raise grapes."

When Seaver gave the terse response, he had already established himself as one of the greatest pitchers to ever pick up a baseball. He is a member of the exclusive 300-win club and was the recipient of three National League Cy Young awards. There were more lucrative ways for one of baseball's all-time legendary players to plan on spending retirement. He could have ventured into commercial investments or corporate speaking tours. (Joe Montana has made an incredibly lucrative career out of the latter option.) Like many superstars, Tom could have built up his personal brand on the national level for marketing and business endeavors. Ultimately, running an unassuming winery business in woodsy Northern California was most appealing-even if it meant waiting a few years.

After retiring from baseball in the late 1980's, Tom Terrific spent his time tending to his lovely home in the posh suburban town of Greenwich, Connecticut. For a while, Seaver was content working on his garden. He made the occasional public appearance at Shea Stadium but for the most part stayed away from flashbulbs and cameras. Dreams morphed into reality in 1998 when the native Californian and longtime wine collector stumbled upon 116 acres of land at Diamond Mountain in Calistoga, California. In the ensuing years a vineyard with 2.5 acres of Cabernet grapes was planted. In 2008, the vineyard garnered national recognition for producing a bottle of 2008 GTS Cabernet Sauvignon that received a top ranking from *Wine Spectator*. Now in his late sixties, Seaver looks forward to producing high quality wines that appear on restaurant menus across America. Coincidentally, he happens to be one of several former notable athletes who have opened up wine vineyards in the West Coast. The first two selected players in the 1993 NFL Draft, Drew Bledsoe and Rick Mirer, operate successful vineyards in Washington and California respectively.

These days Seaver Vineyards is a family run business in every sense of the term. It operates with a small workforce consisting of Tom and his wife Nancy, niece Karen, and a trio of Labradors affectionately known as the Rowdy Boys. There are outside consultants and experts who contribute, but the core of the Vineyard consists of the Seavers and their dogs. Despite battling Lyme disease in recent years, Seaver spends most of his working hours strolling through rows of his vineyard with clippers in hand and dogs behind him. His winery business parallels the understatement and relative solitude that marked his early years of retirement and natural gracefulness that highlighted his playing days.

Several hundred miles north, Shawn Kemp has revitalized his public image and personal well-being by opening a chic restaurant called Oskar's Kitchen, sandwiched between a smoke shop and coffee shop in the Lower Queen Anne section of Seattle. Similar to Seaver, Kemp is very engaged in the fabric of his business. But unlike Seaver, Kemp has channeled his business towards becoming rather intimately engaged with the community in which it is located.

It is understood that Kemp is the owner of the restaurant but that he is not *the* restaurant. On many nights, he is a patron just like any other Seattleite seeking recreation. Kemp stops into his restaurant on a daily basis to chat with the locals and introduce himself to new customers. On some Saturday evenings he will serve as a guest DJ. It is not uncommon to see him pull up a chair alongside customers enjoying lunch on a random Tuesday afternoon. Kemp does not use his basketball legacy to milk more dollars out of his restaurant venture. His name, trademark dunk image, and jersey are nowhere to be found at Oskar's. The scant reference to Kemp is the restaurant's signature drink, the Reignman, a concoction of 151-proof rum, melon liqueur, pineapple juice, and orange juice that has a greenish-yellow color reminiscent of Kemp's Supersonics jersey.

Kemp is the rare superstar athlete who runs a neighborhood business in which he knows customers by name. He was a six-time NBA All-Star who poured in 15,347 career points and at times dominated the paint. Against the Chicago Bulls in the 1996 NBA Finals, Kemp was at the pinnacle of his career and was very much Michael Jordan's equal. Kemp's Sonics fell in six games to the Bulls but their franchise wingman averaged 23.3 points per night. Yet in the post-basketball world of dining and entertainment, Kemp, unlike Jordan, has not run a mega chain restaurant from afar.

On another level, Kemp's re-immersion as a staple of the Seattle community transcends bartending and disc jockeying. It is a throwback to brighter days for many Seattle natives including Kemp. In the 1990's, just as the Supersonics were prospering so too was their host city. During Kemp's reign, Seattle epitomized all that was good about America during the Bill Clinton years. Home prices were soaring, unemployment was microscopic, and computer technology was flourishing. The now defunct KeyArena was the epicenter of such energy. Los Angeles may have had movie stars sitting courtside but Seattle had its unique collection of tech and musical rock stars out in full force for SuperSonics' playoff games. The CEO of Starbucks, Howard Schultz, regularly frequented games before purchasing the team in 2001. At the time, Seattle based businesses such as Microsoft and Starbucks rivaled any of America's behemoth corporations while Kemp and the Sonics could do the same in American basketball. The jewels and gems of the Emerald City sparkled under the KeyArena's roof.

But by the early 2000's, Kemp looked like the poster boy of a superstar athlete falling fast into oblivion. After an incredibly successful career in Seattle, Kemp hit hard times. The final years of his once illustrious career were marked by a peripatetic journey through Cleveland, Portland, and Orlando. Infidelity, weight problems, and drug busts tarnished his formerly dazzling legacy. When the Reignman unceremoniously retired in 2003, he was a mere afterthought in a professional basketball landscape that was being overtaken by the likes of LeBron James, Dwyane Wade, Carmelo Anthony, and Chris Paul.

Simultaneously, the Emerald City would fall from grace. The tech bubble burst and the Sonics moved to the Great Plains to become the Oklahoma City Thunder. It appeared that Grunge Music had reached its apex in the 1990's. The rest of America couldn't overlook the city's stigma of being a rain infested outpost.

But now years later, things are looking brighter. While he may never be remembered as one of the game's true premier power forwards, the restaurant business has saved him personally. It is not just a way to kill time; it has become a full-fledged livelihood. Oskar's serves as Kemp's time machine, allowing him to return to his halcyon days of being a fixture of the Greater Seattle community. And in a sense, it has saved some semblance of Seattle's glory days.

As Kemp told *Sports Illustrated* in July 2012, "Let's be honest, I've gone through some things that made me want to stand up a little taller, stand for something bigger, show a different side. When you make changes in your life, it can be a wonderful thing, you know? I was so afraid of failing. Remember, this was before so many players went right from high school to the NBA, and it was like, if I don't make it, I don't have a degree to fall back on. Even as a rookie I knew that basketball was only going to be a stage, a platform, and I had to have a bigger vision."

Fun and Games

For 12 seasons, Mike Greenwell etched his place in the pantheon of great Boston Red Sox leftfielders alongside Ted Williams, Carl Yastrzemski, Jim Rice, and later Manny Ramirez. A career .303 hitter, Greenwell had his best year in 1988 when he finished runner-up in the MVP voting to embattled slugger Jose Canseco. When the Red Sox eventually called up a promising young leftfielder named Troy O'Leary, Greenwell said goodbye to baseball and the only big league team he had ever played for.

In retirement, the man nicknamed the Gator spends his middle-aged years running his own amusement park, which happens to be in the near vicinity of Fort Myers, Boston's spring training home. Greenwell's 'Bat a Ball and Family Fun Park' spans over 6,000 square feet and sports a 19 Hole Miniature Golf Course, eight batting cages, arcade, and paintball field among other amenities. Since the waning days of Greenwell's playing career, the park has served as an alternative for Floridians who don't have the time and money to trek across state to Disney World. While Greenwell's park obviously lacks the razzle-dazzle of the Magic Kingdom, it serves as a viable diversion for nearby residents who have lived their entire lives in the shadow of a gargantuan cultural institution of commercialized recreation.

Financial Services

The world of investment and finance is in another galaxy compared to that of professional athletics. Spreadsheets and dress suits bear scant resemblance to scorecards and sweatpants. Quantitative analysis involves a very different part of the brain than do the cognitive and motor skills needed for physical dexterity. However, for some pro athletes, the prospect of immersing themselves in a new business venture and networking with new colleagues is more appealing than extending their celebrity status. For athletes who have an intellectual curiosity or natural bent for business, retirement can be a perfect time for exercising such faculties. Those athletes who do move on to the financial services industry are indeed starting over in every sense of the term.

Steve Finley finished with more career hits than either Joe DiMaggio or Mickey Mantle and belted over 300 home runs. Few outfielders were more graceful gliding across vast expanses of grass to snag fly balls. He won Gold Gloves and appeared in multiple World Series and All-Star games. But in 2009, such feats were of little help in getting familiar with LinkedIn and California life insurance exams.

In 2008 Finley called it quits after an illustrious career in which he compiled the aforementioned stats and accolades. For nearly two decades he was one of the game's elite centerfielders. Then younger centerfielders such as Jacoby Ellsbury and Curtis Granderson started taking over. In 2009 Steve embarked on his next career in the insurance industry and since that time he has worked in the business development division of two corporations, Apheta, a life insurance company, and GS Levine Insurance Services, which specializes in property/casualty insurance.

"First two years when I was done playing I just played golf with my friends and my kids. I got bored and one of my close friends who was one of the top insurance agents told me to get my license. It made sense.

"I realize it [professional athletics] is a different world, insulated in the field and clubhouse from realities of business. You live in a fairy tale land. It's eye opening. You realize the politics and the lack of knowledge and networking. I have been on a quick learning curve. It's been very enjoyable. At first not so much but I have learned how to network and I have learned enough about the insurance industry."

Stories of former players going back to school to get their undergraduate and post-graduate degrees don't get enough attention. Many think their fame and riches will automatically translate to business prosperity. Yet poor preparation for business ventures is just as viable of a culprit for financial hardship as is profligacy. For former athletes such as Finley who have the wherewithal and ambition to learn a new craft, the intellectual stimulation can be endlessly rewarding and refreshing.

"I would encourage every athlete who plays a major sport to find something they are interested in outside of sports and also to learn about the business world so that they have something to jump into and have a little background. It's a whole other world out there and there are many business opportunities available," explains Finley.

For athletes nearing retirement, having a fallback plan is necessary for allaying their concerns about sinking when they initially plunge into the choppy waters of post-athletic life. The reality is that financial terms such as assets, liabilities, cash flow, and income statement have very little place in sports competition. Education can be the greatest asset to starting a business.

When Boston Bruins legend Derek Sanderson was in his middle-aged years, he went back to school to learn the fundamentals of business. Few athletes in the history of professional sports have benefitted as much from an education. In retirement, things went from bad to worse in a heartbeat. After skating in his last shift for the Pittsburgh Penguins in the 1977-1978 season, Sanderson had more time for alcoholism and philandering. It didn't take long for him to be so profligate with his money that he was penniless and spent nights sleeping on Central Park benches. Sanderson went from rich to poor virtually overnight and needed to find a new way to make a living.

Sanderson is credited with the assist of Bobby Orr's Stanley Cup series winning goal against the St. Louis Blues on Mother's Day 1970. Later in the decade, Orr assisted Sanderson during his troubled days by encouraging him to go to rehab. After getting back on his feet and broadcasting for a number of years, Sanderson became a Boston based financial advisor, a position that allows him to leverage his financial education towards helping other former athletes prudently manage their finances.

During his playing days, Derek was a star on the ice and partied like one off it. After inking a multi-million dollar contract, Sanderson drove a Rolls Royce, appeared multiple times on the "The Tonight Show," and was named one of the sexiest men in America by *Cosmopolitan* magazine.

Sanderson, along with Bobby Orr, Phil Esposito, and Terry O'Reilly, helped spawn a generation of rabid young hockey fans in Boston. In the 1970's the Bruins were top shelf in Boston sports, winning championships in 1970 and 1972. Sanderson, a friend of Joe Namath's and considered the Joe Namath of hockey, was just as responsible as anyone for helping put hockey on Bostonians' sports map. When the feisty Bruins center was still a young man and playing professional hockey, he could get away with the binge drinking and smoking. His body was still in relatively good shape and there was more than enough money to fund his hedonistic lifestyle. But then he got first-hand experience of what it means for a former athlete to struggle in retirement. His experience serves as the ultimate cautionary tale of recklessness.

In his incredibly candid memoir *Crossing the Line*, Sanderson acknowledged that: "When I was in Boston, I'd been living the life. I was a single guy playing for the most popular team on the planet, beautiful women all around me. The image I projected was that I was a crazy playboy, and I believed my own hype, but the truth was that I was just an insecure kid from Niagara Falls. Because of addiction, fed by ego, the era and more money than I knew what to do with, I was living under bridges, panhandling and eating out of dumpsters six years later."

Similar to Kemp's story, Sanderson's rise to comfort and success has not been a straight line trajectory but rather a sometimes nauseating undulation of hills and valleys. Yet he has come full circle and in his late sixties, serves as a financial advisor to pro athletes. As manager of the Sports Group, a specialized division of Baystate Wealth Management that helps athletes manage their money, Sanderson educates athletes about the importance of long-term financial planning and conservative spending habits.

"I went back to school when I was 50. In 1972 I was the highest paid athlete in the world. This was when cigarettes cost 35 cents. Now it's a different era. I thought it would never end."

Sanderson, who went by the moniker 'Turk' in his playing days, also worked at State Street Global and Howland Capital before working for the Sports Group. Sanderson now helps athletes because he knows they can be vulnerable to unscrupulous agents who often don't negotiate business deals with their clients' best interests in mind. Unlike those who "advised" him during his playing days, Sanderson is not trying to bilk his clients out of hard earned dollars.

"I don't believe in commissions. Commissions are downfall of capitalism. I want to be your friend and make sure you do the right thing."

He is aware that regardless of their pay grade, athletes face grave physical dangers when they check in to work, whether it is facing pucks and baseballs flying over 100 miles per hour or onrushing 250 pound linebackers with bad intentions. While his contemporaries made thousands of dollars playing sports, he harbors no resentment towards the newbies who make millions.

"I wish the current players nothing but the best. They deserve every penny," admits Sanderson. "They still need to pay attention to their investment accounts, what they own, what they are paying for it. They all need to start a plan and stick to a plan. Players make good money these days. If managed properly, they shouldn't have to worry about working when their playing days are done. Athletes as a rule are insecure and overconfident. People forget that the government takes half of what an athlete earns. If he is making $6 million, it means he really is only taking home $3 million. The problem is many of the guys spend as if they've got $10 million. I will not let the players I work with go crazy and buy four cars. And they don't need an 8,000-square foot monument."

However, many of Sanderson's clients are only green in age. They are not signing mega million dollar contracts that will make them independently wealthy for life. What they are doing is signing their first professional contract and in some cases, receiving a lump sum courtesy of their signing bonus.

"It [his managed fund] is a place guys can put their money in when they don't have a lot. It's a beginning vehicle for them. It's a place for beginners, some guys in Minors."

Today Sanderson lives with his wife Nancy in a quiet suburb of Boston. He makes a very nice living and leads a stable life. Most importantly, he is a long way from sleeping on Central Park benches and partying with Joe Namath.

While some such as Sanderson seek to utilize financial services as a vehicle for staying involved in the athletic community, others view it as a means for breaking away.

"I don't find athletes to be as well rounded as I like my business partners to be. They don't understand specifics of business challenges," explained Rich Kelley, a former NBA center who retired from basketball and went on to his get MBA at Stanford. Over the past few decades, Kelley has served as an operator, owner, and investor for various small businesses and start-up companies on the West Coast.

"To be honest, business was not in the back of my mind when I played in the NBA. I came upon the MBA as a safe place to hide myself away, learn about business, costs and benefits of investing. It was a far cheaper tuition than co-signing on a friend's restaurant."

Kelley left the NBA in 1986. The level of isolation between pro athletes and the rest of the world has only grown in leaps and bounds over the past quarter century. Even within the pervasive social media landscape, a seemingly ubiquitous and inviolable barrier separates the athletic pantheon from the general populace. A microscopically miniscule portion of the population can have any kind of substantial access to their athletic heroes who are chauffeured, paraded, and escorted from one venue to the next. While they are receiving such treatment, millions of dollars are being pumped into their bank accounts. Naturally, a feeling of infallibility sets in.

"When you play your sport, you are part of an isolated gypsy tribe; you don't have normal everyday connections to the real world. As an athlete, there is a physical and mental sense of indomitability," acknowledged the former Stanford All-American who co-founded Search Fund Partners, a venture capitalist firm, in 2004.

For that reason, not investing a great deal of one's assets can be a very prudent idea. Rather, investment of time, energy, effort and concentration can be a potential low risk-high reward scenario.

"I wish people could understand that your celebrity opens a lot of doors. You don't have to invest money. You can invest your name and time," explains the seven-foot businessman.

Still not many of Kelley's business partners and competitors can claim they posted up against Magic Johnson or jockeyed for position against Larry Bird in the paint.

"It [having played in the NBA] is part of who I am. I'm not intimidated very often. But world class competition is really in the distant past."

* * *

Aside from the lush monetary rewards, the financial latitude to start a business allows former athletes the opportunity to pursue personal interests in ways that most of us can only dream about. "Succeeding in business" doesn't have to mean earning hundreds of millions of dollars in investments and commercial real estate ventures. Rather, success can be interpreted as putting a creative stamp on your work or learning a new set of skills completely unrelated to sports.

The truth is that there are so many former athletes engaging in business endeavors. This chapter detailed several accounts without even chronicling Charles Oakley's car wash business or wide receiver Wayne Chrebet's financial advisory practice. Hopefully, more professional athletes realize the optimal time to focus on business is during retirement when they can pay their full and undivided attention towards their respective pursuits.

CHAPTER 3
Community Service-Taking a Stand

He may not have been the first star athlete to embrace community service initiatives but no one toiled more tirelessly for the disadvantaged than Roberto Clemente. The son of a sugarcane worker, Clemente came of age in a shoddy wooden dwelling on the backcountry roads of Carolina, Puerto Rico. It didn't take long for professional baseball scouts to realize that he could emerge as a star in the Major Leagues. While becoming the first Hispanic baseball player to reach the ballyhooed milestone of 3,000 hits, Clemente championed efforts to alleviate the suffering of the neglected, oppressed, and impoverished inhabitants of Latin America.

During his time, Clemente was one of the few athletes willing to take a stand against corrupt politicians and rise up to the occasion when natural disasters struck. Shortly after the 1972 season, Clemente received disturbing news reports that the oppressive Nicaraguan army associated with the Somoza government had stolen relief supplies earmarked for the masses of Nicaraguans suffering in the wake of a countrywide earthquake. Coincidentally, Clemente had been visiting the capital city, Managua, three weeks prior to the doomsday earthquake. It didn't matter. He would return in a heartbeat. Clemente took the initiative to get onboard the next supply plane to the ravaged and war torn nation.

While attempting to deliver supplies to survivors on December 31, 1972, the legendary outfielder died in a plane crash. Clemente was immediately enshrined in the Baseball Hall of Fame in Cooperstown, New York, an alcove emblematic of America's pastoral heritage when the autumnal sun emanates on the bucolic town. Had Clemente lived longer, one can only imagine how much he would have helped victims of more recent natural disasters such as the Haitian Earthquake, Hurricane Katrina, and 2004 Tsunami in Southeast Asia. While today's generation of pro athletes is often labeled as selfish and entitled, many have indeed kept alive the fiery spirit of humanitarianism that defined Clemente's heroic life. Whether it is for personal ties or religious purposes, some former pro stars have dedicated their second professional lives towards helping humanity. Most of these stories often elude national coverage and fly under Americans' radar screens. The ensuing pages detail such noble yet often unheralded efforts.

Heart of Poverty

Most Westerners associate the Central African nation of the Congo with Joseph Conrad's literary classic *Heart of Darkness*. The impossibly burdensome lifestyles of the Congolese are often exempt from nightly newscasts and become relegated to mini blurbs deep inside metropolitan newspapers. The facts are rather sobering. The average life expectancy is 42-47 years. In 2003, approximately 2.5% of the population was over 65-years-old. These are numbers that would seem applicable to the Middle Ages, but not the early 21st century. It gets worse. The infant mortality rate in the Congo is 9.6% while nearly 20% of newborn children die before their fifth birthday. In 2002, the Gross Domestic Product (GDP) per capita was merely $600. In comparison, the GDP per capita in the United States was $36,300. In 1995, the country experienced one of the most devastating polio epidemics of the 20th century. Limited to a scarcity of medicinal resources, the Congolese suffered thousands of casualties that could have been avoided with access to modern medicine.

Dikembe Mutombo has been to Central Africa what Clemente was to Central America. The seven-footer, known for his finger wagging and shot blocking, has made it his business to do whatever he can to at least temporarily alleviate the unimaginable suffering afflicted upon so many of his native countrymen. In short, the NBA All-Defensive awards and GEICO commercials merely scratch the surface of Mutombo's fascinating life.

The seventh of 10 children, Dikembe Mutombo Mpolondo Mukamba Jean-Jacques Wamutombo, otherwise known as Dikembe Mutombo, was born in the capital city of Kinshasa in the Democratic Republic of the Congo. He stepped on American soil for the first time in his life in fall 1987 when he began his freshman studies at Georgetown University. Despite his gargantuan size, Mutombo did not get recruited to play on the school's basketball team. His meal ticket to earning a scholarship at one of America's finest universities was his stellar academic track record and accompanying pre-med ambitions. Once it became clear that he had the innate basketball talent to dominate in college and perhaps at the professional level, Mutombo's plans to become a doctor were put on hold. Initially, basketball prevented Mutombo from becoming a doctor who could treat Congolese patients but eventually it provided him with the financial wherewithal to establish a groundbreaking medical center in his native land during the latter portion of his NBA career.

The fruits of Mutombo's labor surfaced on September 15, 2001. When the world was still mourning the 9/11 attacks, Mutombo's foundation unveiled the Biamba Marie Mutombo Hospital and Research Center, the Congo's first modernly equipped hospital since the mid-1900's. Mutombo dedicated the freshly minted 10-acre, 300–bed facility to his late mother. Dikembe contributed over $15 million toward the $29 million hospital building project, hoping that a new facility could effectively diminish the gaping disparity between the healthcare resources available to the Congolese and those accessible to natives of industrialized countries. The center is located in Mutombo's hometown of Kinshasa, a dilapidated and neglected region of the world that he was so fortunate to escape from over a quarter-century ago.

"I came to this beautiful country of the United States of America on a scholarship, which was to go to medical school and one day go home and serve my people. That dream didn't fall apart when I got the chance to play the game of basketball to make money. I was able to use the fortune I made to build this hospital," said Mutombo.

Ann M. Veneman, former Executive Director of UNICEF, has overseen many different initiatives in developing countries and views Mutombo's center as a paradigm for other countries to follow.

"This hospital is an example of what a healthcare system could be like if it were properly implemented throughout the country. It could help to save so many lives, whether it's the children dying of largely preventable causes like malaria, diarrhea, pneumonia, malnutrition. It shouldn't happen," commented Veneman.

Since retiring from the NBA, Mutombo has devoted his professional life towards running the Dikembe Mutombo Foundation, an organization dedicated to improving the lives of the Congolese through providing special care to the nation's poorest residents and training its health professionals with the latest innovative medical devices. In addition to funding the groundbreaking hospital, Mutombo's foundation seeks to disseminate educational information on primary health care matters and disease prevention throughout the Congo.

"I was sick and tired of seeing people dying in the continent of Africa. As a child I saw so many deaths. When I got to the point to be blessed and be put in the shoes God put me in, I felt I had some moral duty to do something in Africa. And I love it. I love it so much. It brings so much joy to me to see that I'm making a difference. We need to build more small clinics all around the continent. Women and children are dying fast because they don't have access to healthcare facilities. People forget about malaria. Malaria is killing more people in the continent of Africa than HIV and AIDS. If you have malaria today and you don't get it treated, in the next 48 hours, you're gone. We have a tendency to shift away from a disease that is taking a toll on our lives. The Old Testament said that people perish because of lack of education."

In college, Mutombo's involvement in noble off court endeavors foreshadowed his mid-life efforts to champion exemplary causes. Even after Georgetown's basketball head coach John Thompson encouraged Mutombo to join the basketball squad, the student-athlete did not waver from his intellectual pursuits. While the Congolese giant did forgo his pre-med track, he graduated Georgetown as a dual major in Linguistics and Diplomacy. Over his collegiate and professional careers, Mutombo has become fluent in nine languages, a handful of which are of an African dialect. Today, Mutombo is a bona fide public figure on the international stage. Aside from his charitable work in his home country, he has become an international spokesperson for human rights and global ambassador of the NBA.

During the waning days of his marathon career, the ferocious shot-blocking center sat next to First Lady Laura Bush while her husband reaped the following praise during his State of the Union Address:

"Dikembe Mutombo grew up in Africa amid great poverty and disease. He came to Georgetown on a scholarship to study medicine. Coach John Thompson took a look at Dikembe and had a different idea. Dikembe became a star in the NBA and a citizen of the United States but he never forgot the land of his birth or the duty to share his blessings with others. A friend has said of this good hearted man that Mutombo believes God has given him this opportunity to do great things. And we're proud to call this son of the Congo a citizen of the United States of America."

A rousing applause lasting nearly half a minute ensued for one of the world's great humanitarians.

Cleaning up City Streets

Before he was manning the low post for the San Antonio Spurs in the 1990's, David Robinson was the epitome of class. During a time when star high school basketball players were starting to go straight to the NBA, Robinson opted to prolong his college experience for the sake of public service. That meant he was the rarest of rare: a basketball star for the Navy Midshipmen. Fittingly, his moniker during his NBA career was "the Admiral," a name he acquired because of his time at the Naval Academy, where he studied math and engineering. Robinson's postponement of his NBA career for Navy service bears some resemblance to Ted Williams' decision to give up several of his prime years to fly combat missions over the Pacific Ocean during World War II. When he retired as a member of the San Antonio Spurs, he was recognized by the NBA as one of the 50 greatest players in league history.

"My experience as a student athlete really has affected the way that I live today, especially at the Naval Academy where there is a strong sense of service," explains Robinson. "We went there knowing that we were joining the military and if we needed to lay our lives down for our country-that was what we were going to do. Everything we did there reinforced that thought and when I came out, I just wanted to make my community better. The community of San Antonio had been so kind to me. I just wanted to make the community stronger."

As one of the rare franchise players to play his entire career in the same city, Robinson naturally developed a strong affinity to San Antonio. The reality is that when he lived in San Antonio during basketball season, he spent half the time travelling on road trips. Retirement is the optimal time to be engaged in the San Antonio community.

David also knew how to represent his country. After playing on the 1992 Dream Team in Barcelona, Robinson was one of the few members who joined the 1996 U.S. Olympic Team, which also won a gold medal at the Summer Games in Atlanta. The next NBA season, Robinson would face the gravest challenge of his career. The Admiral suffered a back injury prior to the 1996-1997 season and returned to play in six games before fracturing his left foot. The Spurs slumped to 20-62 that year, but the silver lining for the Silver and Black team was a chance to select first in the 1997 Draft. As the hackneyed expression goes, sometimes it is better to be lucky than good. Thanks to the pre-draft lottery, the Spurs were positioned to select Robinson's heir apparent and a once-in-a-generation player, Wake Forest power forward Tim Duncan.

Despite missing virtually one year due to injury and joining the league late, Robinson was still able to win two championships while helping Duncan develop into a superstar. Rare is the veteran who has the humility to submerge his will for the betterment of the team. Robinson would spend the latter part of his career mentoring Duncan, a fellow frontcourt star who would lead the Spurs to multiple world championships in the early 21st century.

For a former Dream Teamer, NBA champion, and Hall of Famer, Robinson has kept a relatively low profile in retirement. He does not appear in primetime commercials or play cameo roles in hit television shows. Rather than flaunting his celebrity status in publicity laden endeavors, Robinson has devoted his professional life towards spearheading sustainable community improvement projects.

In 2002, Robinson started Carver Academy, a five acre kindergarten through sixth grade private school built in a neighborhood formerly burdened by hideous urban blight and rampant drug handling. The school, which serves dozens of underprivileged children, is named after George Washington Carver, a botanist and educator whose discoveries revolutionized Southern agriculture. Born into slavery, Carver earned multiple degrees before discovering hundreds of uses for pecans, soybeans, and sweet potatoes.

Robinson founded the school with a simple mission: to provide disadvantaged children with the same quality of an education that children in upper-middle class communities are accustomed to receiving. From Robinson's perspective, unequal access to education breeds an exponentially growing achievement gap.

"I would see a lot of kids, while traveling with the NBA, that wanted to be an NBA player or a rapper, and I thought that was just terrible. I want them to get an education first, and then they can go on and do whatever they want to with their lives. Giving back is so important for me I think because it's investing in the next generation. If I can build into the life of a young kid, or a young family, I'm a part of their life forever," the admirable Robinson commented.

Since its inception, the school has been a remarkable success. Classes do not exceed 15 students. School violence has become virtually non-existent. Due in large part to Robinson's initial $10 million donation, approximately 95 percent of Carver students receive some form of financial aid. In addition to providing the financial head start, Robinson assumed a very hands-on role in the daily operations of the school through raising money for scholarships and facility upgrades including a mixed media room and state-of-the-art library. The Admiral would personally oversee the development of the curriculum and onboarding of new hires. Consistent with the understated elegance that marked his playing career, there has not been one semblance of his basketball legacy in any corner of the school.

In addition to his community activism, Robinson has maintained a visible presence at youth athletic events. One of his sons is a gifted wide receiver who earned a football scholarship to Notre Dame. During his high school football games, the elder Robinson frequently volunteered to grill hot dogs at concession stands for surprised fans.

Robinson's retirement reflects the graceful manner in which he exited from the NBA. While many star athletes don't know when to leave, Robinson was the exception. He left on top, helping the San

Antonio Spurs win another NBA Championship in 2003 by defeating the New Jersey Nets. In the series clinching Game 6 victory, Robinson tallied 13 points and hauled in 17 rebounds for another one of his trademark double doubles. *Sports Illustrated* tabbed Robinson and Duncan as their sportsmen of the year in 2003. It was a seamless passing of the baton from one living legend to another.

That same year, Mo Vaughn, another star athlete who would later embark on community activism, decided to call it quits. Their departures from sports could not have been any more different. Whereas Robinson rode off into the Texas sunset as a hero, Vaughn bowed out in a fairly nondescript fashion. A former American League All-Star and MVP, Vaughn saw his career spiral downwards ever since he left the friendly confines of Fenway Park. Following the 1998 season in Boston, one in which Vaughn was constantly bickering with Red Sox management over contract extensions, he bolted westward to the franchise formerly known as the Anaheim Angels. After agreeing to a six-year contract worth $82 million in the offseason, Vaughn started his career with the Angels by tearing multiple ligaments in his ankle after chasing down a pop fly on opening night. He was never the same-to put it mildly. As his weight soon surpassed his batting average, the Angels had no choice but to deal Vaughn to the Mets during the dog days of the 2001 season. Injuries and weight issues would continue to plague Vaughn throughout his tenure with the Mets, leaving him with no choice but to retire in 2003.

It would have been easy for Vaughn to have an unproductive retirement period. He was living in New York City with career earnings north of $100 million. A surplus of money and time was on his side. Trouble could have easily found him as it so often did earlier in his career. A history of off-field mishaps including an intoxicated driving incident and public fight had dogged Vaughn during his Boston years. Yet in retirement, Mo is once again having a positive influence, just as he did during much of his time in Boston. As a player, Vaughn, along with teammates John Valentin and Tim Wakefield, were champions of the Jimmy Fund. As a retiree, Vaughn has again devoted a significant portion of his daily life towards helping those in dire need.

His real estate company, Omni New York LLC, has established a vibrant presence in New York City's low income housing community by managing over 4,000 apartment units for recipients of Section 8 rent subsidies. In a metropolis often associated with the gilded cocoons of the wealthy, Omni has garnered a reputation for transforming properties once deemed untouchable in the Big Apple's caste system of real estate.

Vaughn joined with his lawyer Eugene Schneur and businessman Robert Bennett to establish the firm in 2004. The triumvirate has focused on acquisition rehabs — purchases of older properties that are withering away in decrepitude due to the negligence of landlords. Vaughn and his colleagues have hired construction crews to patch gaping holes, mend leaky ceilings, and install new lights and utilities as a means of refurbishing the city's most dilapidated and economically distressed housing complexes. Some of the most notable acquisitions have included Noble Drew Ali Plaza, Thessalonica Court, and Brookhaven Apartments. Neighborhoods where drug dealers once sold cocaine alongside malnourished pit bulls are now home to residential areas where people can find affordable shelter during the brutally cold winter months.

Running Back Home

Sadly for far too many Americans, the American Dream remains just that-a dream. They can never save up enough money to afford a down payment on a piece of property that they call their own. Rather than build up equity, such hard working folks see a good portion of their paychecks go to rent, helping a landlord build up his or her equity and personal net worth. Warrick Dunn, the same Warrick Dunn who rushed for over 10,000 yards in the NFL and earned All-American honors at Florida State, has devoted his post-football days to helping some Americans avoid that sad fate.

Like the beneficiaries of his foundation, Dunn had to work for everything in his life. He made the most of his 5'10" frame and humble background. His mother had to raise a family on her own by working multiple jobs. By the time Dunn was a senior in high school it looked like his prospects were brightening. He had multiple scholarship offers from some of the top collegiate football programs in the country. The feeling among scouts, coaches, and other talent evaluators was that as long as Dunn stayed relatively healthy, his immense talents would punch his ticket to a career in the NFL. But just as such hopeful promises were coming to fruition, a nightmarish phone call jolted Dunn's world.

On the night of January 7, 1993, Dunn's mother, Betty Smothers, was shot and killed during an armed robbery at a local bank. The cruel irony is that one of Smothers' jobs was working as a Baton Rouge police officer to help keep her community safe. Unfortunately, Dunn is far from the only professional athlete to endure such a challenging upbringing. However, the manner in which he has given back to others has been very unique. Dunn has kept his mother's dream of owning a home alive with his spectacular charitable program called Homes for the Holidays Foundation. For the past decade, Dunn's program has helped dozens of single parents become first-time homeowners as it contributes funds towards down payments and furnishes the houses with food, furniture, garden tools, televisions, and computers. Their hard earned paychecks don't just go towards bills and taxes. It now also goes towards something they own.

"The first five years it was just a program. It was hard to understand the commitment it takes for a foundation," explains Dunn. "I felt like if you sustain something and see it through, you really need to get behind it. It's my baby but it's my mom's idea and her dream.

To be passionate about that-you need to go out and give everything you have."

Dunn was not born with tremendous size but pound for pound, he was one of the NFL's most explosive offensive players during the late 1990's and early 2000's. The Tampa Bay Buccaneers and Atlanta Falcons were blessed to have one of the most durable and productive running backs in the league's history. He absorbed bruising hits from linebackers yet missed hardly any games over a 12-year career. Dunn, the 12th overall pick in the 1997 NFL Draft, tallied 10,967 rushing yards and 49 touchdowns while earning three Pro Bowl nods.

Dunn was fortunate to be one of many young men who played for former head coach Tony Dungy, the rare NFL team boss who doesn't believe in yelling or cursing at his players. The only time he gets visibly upset is when players disregard community activities. Like many rookies, Dunn felt Dungy's paternal influence from the get-go.

"I got the idea when I was challenged by Tony Dungy when I was a rookie," explains Dunn. "He said how if you live in a community you need to be a part of it. I had to think about what was going on in my community and what I was passionate about. We started tossing around ideas. All I could think about was my mom and her dreams of home ownership. She never had that opportunity. I did some research and we did three homes that first year. I didn't understand what I was doing, what I was getting into, the magnitude of it. I went home that night, saw it on the news, and thought 'wow that was pretty cool.' I wanted to maintain it. It has just taken off. I think of my mom and the things she went through to put food on the table and a roof over our heads."

The people who benefit from Dunn's foundation are those who demonstrate a sustainable desire to be self-sufficient. Like Dunn, they were not given anything. They are afforded an advance on their home only after they have proven capable of holding down a job, paying bills, and caring for loved ones. These are not free riders but the worthiest of worthy.

"We find people who are that hungry for having a stable environment, a place where they can lay their heads down at night and provide a better environment for kids and a place for the future. We do all the things for filling the homes. We even put apple pies on the table. They have to earn this right, prove that they are worthy of this. Many families we have helped have gone out and gotten to that point in life. So many people struggle and made some mistakes early. We all make bad mistakes. Hopefully we can put it together.

"People say I should be an expert at housing but the one thing I have learned over the years is you really appreciate what you earn, whether it's proof for a loan, maintaining a job, sweating equity for a home. That's proven sustainable. We give them a fresh start that's what we do."

His foundation primarily helps families in the Baton Rouge, Tampa, Tallahassee, and Atlanta areas who "get to that point where they can't get over the hump." His allegiance has remained strong to the Deep South but the hope is that the program's brilliant successes will percolate across different regions of the country.

"Coming from Louisiana, I fell in love with the South. In the North it gets freezing cold. I like the nature of the people in the South, everyone's nice. Being from Louisiana, we speak to each other all the time, even if we don't know each other. The South is near and dear to my heart. We want to try to expand the program in the South, other parts of the country."

Even in retirement, Dunn is right up there with Chipper Jones, Ted Turner, and Ludacris in being one of the most notable public figures in Atlanta. His connections have helped catapult Homes for the Holidays to great success. But Warrick knows it doesn't have to be that way. A charity does not need the backing of a celebrity to serve its purpose.

"It [charitable work] can be an everyday person. Find what you are passionate about, a cause you can get behind. It's not let me go start a charity. If someone else is doing good work, you should want to partner. You can get it to another level."

* * *

When they are playing, nearly all professional athletes in one of the four major sports at least dabble into some charity work. While it is often mandatory in their contracts, most genuinely embrace helping the less fortunate and becoming immersed in the communities which they represent on game day. When sports are over, community service can become a full-fledged career as it has for many.

CHAPTER 4
From Fans to Constituencies

It would be an understatement to say that not many athletes make it onto both the covers of *TIME* Magazine and *Sports Illustrated*. Generally speaking, business and political dignitaries have their place on the former while the latter is the domain of athletes. Rarely does a sports figure or issue grace the cover of one of the world's most visibly prestigious magazines such as *TIME*. Hall of Fame New York Knicks guard Bill Bradley would be the exception.

The October 4, 1999 issue of *TIME* pictured Bradley with the headline: "The Man Who Could Beat Gore." At the time, the New Jersey Senator was vying for the Democratic Presidential Nomination. Months later he would eventually lose to Vice-President Al Gore in what turned out to be a fairly lopsided race. The fact that Bradley-- who devoted the better part of his twenties and thirties to athletics and not politics or law--had a fighting chance for the presidency speaks to his uniquely versatile makeup.

Several decades earlier, a 1968 *Sports Illustrated* cover pictured Bradley with the headline: "How Good?" As a rookie for the Knicks, Bradley played alongside basketball legends Willis Reed and Walt Frazier after he manned the Princeton backcourt the prior winter. For his career, Bradley amassed over 9,000 career points and 2,500 assists. He would play his entire NBA career for the Knicks before transitioning to another lofty post in the tri-state region.

It is mind-boggling how much one person has accomplished in a single lifetime. It is debatable whether he is better known as a politician, athlete, world class scholar, or public spokesperson. From 1979 to

1997 he served in the U.S. Senate. In 2000 he went up against Gore for the Democratic Nomination for U.S. President. He helped the New York Knicks win two world championships before being elected to the NBA Hall of Fame in 1982. He holds a B.A. degree in American History from Princeton University and an M.A. degree from Oxford University where he was a Rhodes Scholar. Bradley would defy the ridiculously false and outdated stereotype of the "dumb jock," proving gifted athletes can still possess the gift of great intellectualism.

The specific article from the aforementioned *TIME* issue was called "The Art of Being Bradley." Writer Eric Pooley made the following astute observations about one of the most accomplished Americans of our life time: "He is a calculating man who approaches campaigning the way he approached basketball: by analysis and repetition, breaking every shot and move down to its component parts, then mastering them. He had to figure out who he was and what he wanted--choosing Princeton over basketball powerhouse Duke, for example, because Princeton graduated more Rhodes Scholars and he wanted to go to Oxford. Playing for the Knicks was a standing invitation to the round-the-clock bash that was Manhattan in the late 1960s and early '70s, but Bradley did not partake. He kept his head in his books."

Like other athletes who venture into politics, there is some crossover between being a public figure in the athletic arena and one in the political arena. Handshakes, high-fives, smiles, and autographs are standard fare for entering both professions.

"Bradley can interact warmly with strangers, flatter business moguls with disarming questions about their lives, yet never quite lose his proud reserve, a diffidence stoked by 40 years of stardom in sport and politics," explained Pooley.

To date, no former athlete has quite garnered Bradley's national level of political prestige, at least not yet. While former athletes cannot all leverage immense personal wealth towards running a campaign, many do have the public visibility factor in their favor. Some are grizzled veterans while others are rising stars in the political arena but their collective experiences show that parallels do exist between the two lines of work.

Point Guard Mayors

Kevin Johnson may not have been a Hall of Famer, but few NBA stars were as impressive to watch with the basketball in their hands as KJ was in the 1990's. A wizard on the hard court, Johnson dazzled teammates and opponents with his pinpoint precision passing. He could also score, averaging 17.9 points per game over an illustrious 13-year NBA career. Johnson's watershed moment came during the 1992-1993 season when he served as Charles Barkley's sidekick in helping revitalize the Phoenix Suns franchise en route to a 62-win season and NBA Finals appearance.

Similar to Bradley, Johnson was also a former point guard who gravitated to politics after putting aside his basketball sneakers. Kevin Johnson, or KJ as he was affectionately known to his fans, was elected as the 55th mayor of the City of Sacramento in November 2008 before being re-elected to a second term in June 2012. He is the first native of Sacramento and the first African-American to be elected to that post. November 2008 was the same election season when another young African-American man was elected to a high political office. Similarities abound between Johnson and the newly elected Commander in Chief, Barack Obama. Both candidates were raised by their Caucasian maternal grandparents, developed a passion for nonprofit educational movements, and ultimately rose to political stardom despite humble beginnings. And for different reasons, both had their full and undivided attention on the Chicago Bulls during June 1993. Obama is a devout Bulls fan and the Suns almost knocked off the Bulls in what was one of the greatest NBA Finals series of all-time. To this day, the two remain in constant contact.

"There are a lot of similarities between politics and sports," says Johnson. "When I played in the NBA, people threw elbows down in the paint. Politics is a contact sport. The elbows are even sharper in politics. The other thing is when you play basketball, and I'm a point guard, you've got 12 teammates, 11 teammates, and they all want the ball. And they all have big egos so you have to figure out a way to keep everybody happy. In politics, it's the same way. You've got constituents; it's a lot more than 12. They all have their interests. And you as an elected official have to figure out a way to keep everybody satisfied."

At times serving as a politician is a mission impossible task, akin to guarding Michael Jordan or Magic Johnson. The results won't be perfect. All your constituents or fans can ask is that you leave it all on the political or hard court floor. There will always be critics but at the end of the day there is an inherent satisfaction in knowing that at least some portion of the public is impressed with the fruits of your labor.

Johnson's Suns were a perennial opponent to the Sacramento Kings, a Western Conference foe. Some guys coach for the teams they used to compete against as players. Very few serve as mayors for the host cities of such opposing teams. Through serving as mayor of Sacramento, Johnson has spent thousands of hours helping a city that used to consider him an adversary. In 2013, Johnson proved as influential as any public figure in salvaging the franchise still known as the Sacramento Kings. As a player, Johnson played a leading role in preventing the Kings from winning a division title; as a politician, Johnson made sure the team would stay in Sacramento. In the beginning of his second term, he forged a key partnership with software tycoon Vivek Ranadive to construct a new $448 million arena for the Sacramento Kings as part of a larger attempt to redevelop the Downtown Plaza area.

At the beginning of his first term, KJ had his hands full when he assumed his mayoral duties. Sacramento is not as sprawling of a metropolis as Los Angeles, San Diego, or San Francisco but it is, after all, the capital of California, which comprises one of the largest economies in the world. During the dark days of the Great Recession, Sacramento was riddled with a bevy of seemingly insurmountable problems including an overreliance on government jobs, an unbalanced economy, and rampant foreclosures. As a first term mayor, Johnson led Sacramento on a fast break to successfully rebounding from the depths of the recession. The Phoenix Suns legend made it his personal mission as mayor to make Sacramento "a city that works for everyone." Some of his more impressive initiatives have included: Volunteer Sacramento, For Arts Sake, Sacramento Steps Forward, Standup, and Sacramento READS! His administration helped secure over a half billion dollars of federal aid to stimulate the local economy. His Sacramento First Initiative generated over 4,000 new jobs while subsequently bolstering the city's infrastructure. For good reason, public safety, job growth, environmental sustainability, and public education reform were buzzwords that characterized Johnson's first term as Sacramento mayor. In the history of California's capital city, few Sacramento governmental officials had done so much with so little. Johnson earned a well-deserved re-election bid in 2012.

"When you think of being an elected official you think about the negatives and the challenges that go with it but the positives far outweigh it. For every one shortcoming that comes with the job, there are ten things that are much more positive. There's nothing I'd rather be doing," Johnson exclaimed in the midst of his second term.

Like many recently retired athletes, Johnson was never an elected official before becoming mayor. He majored in political science at the University of California Berkeley but never had working experience in politics. Like so many first time politicians, he had to learn on the fly.

"The last time I ran for anything was third grade when I was class president. The interesting thing is if you're successful in one area, a lot of the same skills and characteristics will transfer into another area. As a rookie, as a mayor I made a lot of mistakes. There's this constant cycle of learning. I think all effective leaders are never going to be at a point where they don't learn anymore."

Similar to how he was as a basketball player, Johnson remains cool, calm, and collected as a politician. He is not one for articulating messages via railing diatribes or fire-and-brimstone speeches. For the most part, bickering and finger pointing are not part of his political game plan. Rather, his leading by example mantra has yielded sustainable improvements for his fellow Californians to observe firsthand. One of basketball's most gifted ball handlers has toiled tirelessly and successfully to instill a sense of regional pride in Sacramento denizens.

"Part of the reason I ran for mayor was that I wanted to bring something new to local government. I wanted to be very transparent. I wanted to create an environment that people felt empowered. I wanted to create an environment where people could hold their elected officials accountable. What happens in Washington and the state of California, it trickles down to Sacramento even if it did not directly originate in my city."

During the depths of the 2008 Global Financial Crisis, Sacramento was a fairytale land compared to Detroit, a city whose recent mayor was another basketball legend, Dave Bing. The Motor City has epitomized the downside of de-industrialization and globalization. Urban blight has pervaded what was once a proud bastion of middle class financial stability. At the dawn of the 21st century, Detroit was already saddled with an endless string of financial burdens. Factories closed down because their jobs opened overseas. Real estate values plummeted to frighteningly unforeseen levels. The city's world-renowned automotive industry was dying in front of Detroiters' weary eyes. Weeded lots and abandoned buildings were entrenched in the city's decrepit landscape. At the beginning of the 2009 season, Detroit Tigers manager Jim Leyland told his players that this was not the summer to forget about running out ground balls. Amidst rampant unemployment and underemployment, Detroiters who could scrounge enough money up for a ballgame deserved to see multi-million dollar athletes hustle down to first base.

Shortly after Johnson and Obama started serving their fellow Americans, Bing assumed arguably the hardest political position on the planet when he was named Detroit's new mayor. Raised by a housekeeper and bricklayer in a working class Washington, D.C. neighborhood, Bing was elected mayor of Detroit on May 5, 2009. A political novice, Dave was elected to serve the remainder of Kwame M. Kilpatrick's mayoral term. Kilpatrick was a smooth-talking, larger-than-life politician who ended up resigning and serving jail time for obstruction of justice after covering up an extramarital affair with his chief of staff.

Whereas Johnson was born and raised in Sacramento, Bing was a part of Detroit's legacy because he starred for the Detroit Pistons in the 1970's. Similar to Johnson, Bing was a rookie embarking on a whole new career in the game of politics after enjoying veteran status in pro basketball for so many years. In the NBA, Bing was not just a very good player. He was a great one. Over the course of his sparkling 12-year career, Bing averaged over 20 points and six assists per game while garnering seven NBA All-Star appearances. He was even tabbed the All-Star Game's Most Valuable Player in 1976. Anointed one of the 50 greatest players in NBA history, Bing deservedly earned a spot in the Basketball Hall of Fame. Yet to modern day Detroit residents, Bing's greatest purpose in life may very well be his herculean efforts to revitalize the city they call home.

"I know the reason I took this position is to make the hard decisions so that this city would have a future. It's probably the second most difficult job in this country behind the President of the United States," acknowledged Bing.

Having been the face of the Detroit Pistons franchise for a good deal of the 1960's and 1970's, Bing knows very well the nightmarish transformation that has recently overtaken Motown. In his earlier years, Bing didn't just immerse himself in the athletic sphere of Detroit life and culture. While holding down the backcourt for the Pistons in the seventies, Bing felt inclined to become more educated about the mortgage and loan business, as he was in the midst of applying for his first mortgage. Akin to a college student having a summer internship, Bing spent eight consecutive summers serving as a management trainee for the National Bank of Detroit. He knew his basketball career had a looming expiration date. Summer was the time for learning a new craft as a means of preparing for the inevitable life after hoops.

In an interview with the *Washington Post* several years back, Bing admitted that even before athletes made millions upon millions of dollars, "the mistake most of us make is that we think we're going to play forever. Very few guys, I think, prepare for a second career. The lifestyle we lead and the position that the public puts us in as a successful athlete make us think we're invincible."

Bing played in an era when a superstar's annual salary such as his did not eclipse $225,000. He needed to pursue non-basketball endeavors in order to become wealthy. Soon after his basketball career wrapped up in 1978, Bing worked for two years at Paragon Steel. Initially, the corporation was interested in hiring a former basketball star to serve as an iconic PR figure. Bing had no use for such superficiality; he wanted to learn the ins and outs of the steel business, an industry that was at the epicenter of the city he proudly represented for years. After working in Paragon's Marketing, Accounting, Sales, and Inventory Control Departments, Bing felt ready to jumpstart his own business--but not without reservations. At the time Bing candidly acknowledged to the *Black Enterprise* magazine that: "Most folks don't think blacks understand economies of scale, big business and big dollars. There were people who didn't think I had the ability or acumen to understand that. Secondly, being an athlete was a negative [thing], because we are viewed as idiots."

Bing Group started out as an auto supply outfit with four workers and $180,000 in loans and personal funds. Before the former backcourt wizard sold Bing Group in 2009, the business had generated over $300 million in sales. Bing had the financial wherewithal to run a political campaign and commit full-time hours to serving as a politician. He also had the patience and humility to get ready for an impending smorgasbord of headaches and obstacles. Upon becoming mayor, Bing knew that he would have to make do with the scarcity of resources at his disposal.

"Detroit was a booming, thriving city. It was the automotive capital of the world. I mean, dominated by the Big Three, General Motors, Ford, and Chrysler. Motown was still here when I got here. Over time things started to change. Motown left the city. The automotive industry started to go down. Our population when I first got here was 1.3, 1.4 million. Now, it's about 700,000 people. And so you've got a city that's got about 138 square miles that you could fit Manhattan, Boston, and San Francisco in and we've got 700,000 people. So we've got this infrastructure without the revenue to give the people their services."

For a neophyte in politics, Bing fared pretty well considering he entered what was virtually a no-win situation. In his first and only term as mayor of Detroit, Bing jumpstarted the Detroit Youth Violence Prevention Initiative in an attempt to stem the meteoric upsurge of gang related violence that has plagued the Motor City. Under Bing's watch, Detroit Blight Authority, a public-private partnership, made great strides in demolishing vacant and dilapidated structures near public school districts. New recreation center programs and a state-of-the-art Public Safety Headquarters highlight the city's slowly but steadily improving infrastructure. There are signs of life thanks in no small part to Bing's painstaking efforts.

Ultimately, he found that politics is like basketball in the sense that no individual person can get it done on his or her own. The key is to surround oneself with trustworthy teammates who believe in reciprocity and work in concert to achieve a mutual goal. Unfortunately, Bing didn't have the right supporting cast during his tenure as Motor City mayor. He could deal with a dwindling population and shrinking economy, but not with the distractions of a City Council hesitant to embrace his plans for radical change or Michigan Governor Rick Snyder appointing an emergency manager hell bent on usurping power to modify contracts and sell key municipal assets.

During a May 2013 press conference held at the Charles H. Wright Museum of African-American History, Bing made some tersely pointed remarks justifying his decision to not run for a second term:

"The city was in pain when we came on board and it pained me to see it in this condition. We could accomplish so much more if we just work together. Our citizens need the City Council to help move the city forward, not become a stumbling block to progress. They need to be held accountable."

As Bing approaches his seventies, stepping down from one of the most demanding and tormenting political jobs in the universe makes perfect sense. When he declared his exit from the mayoral post, Bing hinted that he may be interested in running for office at some point in the future. Irrespective of his next move, few individuals have had such a profound and diverse influence on Detroit for nearly half a century.

Battling in the Mid-Atlantic Trenches

The plight of blue-collar workers toiling for their sliver of the American Dream is a common motivator for many who choose to run for political office. Such financial hardships were not lost on former Philadelphia Eagles offensive lineman Jon Runyan when he retired from the NFL and journeyed on to a fresh new career in public service. Similar to Bing, Runyan has deep roots in Michigan's automotive industry. Born in Flint, Michigan, Runyan grew up in a family whose primary breadwinner was his father, a General Motors employee. Runyan personally knew about the pain inflicted upon so many honest blue-collar auto workers who were laid off and unable to afford summer vacations up in the Northern Michigan lakes. Now as a politician, Runyan knows that public funds and efforts can revitalize private industry if they are earmarked in an efficient and appropriate manner.

Runyan came of age in the NFL at the dawn of a new era--at least for offensive linemen such as himself. On February 14, 2000, Runyan signed a six-year, $30 million contract, at the time the largest contract for the largest sized members of an NFL roster. Over the past couple decades, owners have realized that the offensive tackle is as valuable an asset as any on their rosters and thus they deserve to be compensated accordingly. During the 2013 NFL Draft, three of the top four picks were offensive linemen. Team executives could not forget Lawrence Taylor's excruciatingly violent and career derailing hit on Washington Redskins quarterback Joe Theismann. An NFL franchise's most prized possession, the star quarterback, warrants first-rate protection from a behemoth and deftly skilled offensive lineman.

Despite the landmark contract for an offensive lineman, Runyan didn't play like an entitled multi-million-dollar star. He epitomized Philadelphians' blue-collar attitude with his grit and toughness. He was a true ironman for the Philadelphia Eagles, not missing a single game from 2000-2008 when he donned the city's beloved green and black garb. For years, he had the weight of a football crazed city on his broad shoulders as he was solely responsible for protecting franchise quarterback Donovan McNabb's blindside. The Eagles would not have made it to a string of NFC Championship games without Runyan's invaluable services at the line of scrimmage.

In his post-football years, he continues to serve the Mid-Atlantic region, this time as a representative for the 3rd District of New Jersey. Runyan is one of four former NFL players to be elected to

Congress, the other three being Jack Kemp, Steve Largent, and Heath Shuler. Runyan won the 3rd District seat when he ousted Democratic incumbent John Adler in the November 2010 state election. Like many aspiring politicians, Runyan was fortunate to have the financial resources to embark on a full-fledged campaign.

His campaign for a Seat in the House was a crash course in politics. His personal inclinations were towards ensuring that government spends funds in a prudent and selective manner. He harbored serious doubts about the landmark overhaul of national health care, believing such an initiative was an example of government overstepping its boundaries. At the onset of his campaign, Runyan didn't back down from speaking his mind on how he felt Washington was flawed.

"I don't think that the way that Washington is approaching it right now, by spending another big spending bill, they're going to end up raising taxes -- that doesn't need to be done," the former All-Pro lineman told a gaggle of New Jersey reporters during his campaign.

While Runyan made his conservative inclinations relatively clear soon after he announced his candidacy, he also had to bear in mind that his district, which spans across Southern New Jersey from the Philadelphia suburbs to the shore, often leans towards the middle. Ultimately, Runyan struck the right balance in the eyes of potential voters to prove victorious during the 2010 midterm election. His victory came on the same night that two former NBA centers, Chris Dudley and Shawn Bradley, lost their bids for Oregon governor and Utah legislator respectively.

Since Runyan's victorious night in early November 2010, New Jersey has experienced some trying times during his Congressional stewardship--no more so than fall 2012 when Hurricane Sandy wreaked havoc on the Eastern seaboard. Amidst the nearly apocalyptic conditions, Runyan helped New Jersey residents in the same workmanlike fashion in which he protected quarterbacks from onrushing linebackers. He partnered with fellow heavyweight New

Jersey politician Chris Christie to help New Jersey residents get back on their feet following one of the worst national disasters to ever ravage the East Coast. Runyan was influential in pushing forth the Hurricane Sandy Tax Relief Act that would provide financial assistance for alleviating the burdensome losses incurred due to Hurricane Sandy. There was a particular emphasis on providing tax breaks for Jersey Shore businesses to recuperate and hire adequate help to be up and running for the following summer. Runyan bought into the ethos of colleagues on both sides of the aisle collaborating for the sake of the public good.

Like many current and former NFL players, Runyan has taken a particular interest in helping veterans become more financially comfortable upon transitioning back to the home front. A disturbing 2012 report from the VA's Board of Veterans Appeals noted that the Veterans Affairs Office takes three quarters of a year to process disability benefits compensation claims. The turnaround timeframe for the department's claims appeal decisions can drag out for three full years. Like many politicians, Runyan is in politics to rectify an egregious injustice; he believes that politics can transcend needlessly overcomplicated bureaucratic ineptitude. Runyan has taken great pride in chairing the Subcommittee on Disability Assistance and Memorial Affairs (DAMA), believing that the committee can make great strides in expediting the cumbersome and drawn-out appeals process regarding disability benefits claims for the Department of Veterans Affairs.

"Since coming to Congress, fixing the veterans' claims backlog has been one of my top priorities," acknowledged Runyan. "It is unacceptable that our veterans, who have sacrificed so much to protect our nation, are forced to wait years before they are offered a decision on their appeals claim."

While Runyan gets immense satisfaction from helping storm ravaged victims and war-torn veterans, he has publicly said politics may not be his last career. As a relatively young man in his early forties, Runyan is leaving the door open to pursue other interests later in life. But for now, Congressional work in Southern New Jersey perfectly suits his temperament and priorities. Whereas he used to serve the Pennsylvania/New Jersey region on NFL Sundays, he is now doing so on every other day of the week as a politician.

* * *

Politics can be a terrific career for athletes who always remembered that they were representing the name on the front of their jersey and not the one on the back. Both careers allow one to be a community representative, albeit in a very different fashion. Shortly after a team wins a championship, its players get to meet the president during an honorary ceremony at the White House. Maybe one day they will be meeting a president who has been in their athletic shoes.

CHAPTER 5
Showtime

When he was playing for the Oakland A's, the endlessly controversial slugger Jose Canseco once barged into his manager's office. His manager, Tony La Russa, had taken issue with Canseco's showboating antics and rock star persona. Canseco justified his histrionics of admiring homeruns and kissing his biceps in the name of being an entertainer first, athlete second. From Canseco's perspective, sports was merely one other facet of entertainment, just like movies, music, and theater. First and foremost, he believed he was a performer, the one who was supposed to hit 500-foot home runs as a means of bedazzling paying spectators. Traditionalists crave the hit and run but as the saying goes, chicks dig the long ball. No one knows for certain how the altercation resolved itself, but it is understood that the two baseball lifers had a fundamental disagreement over what constitutes a professional athlete.

In his lightning rod of an autobiography called *Juiced*, Canseco made the following comment to at least partially justify his flamboyant behavior and steroid use: "I was an entertainer, I knew it, and I never had a problem with it. I've always considered myself that way. I've always told the media we're all entertainers, or should be, anyway."

Off the field, Canseco took advantage of being an American celebrity by partying with other hotshots and even dating one of the country's biggest pop stars of the time, Madonna. To justify blowing off pre-game batting practice Canseco once told his manager: "I was at Madonna's house, talking to her, and I'm late. So I missed batting practice." Interestingly, a decade later, another wildly controversial slugger, Alex Rodriguez, would have a romantic fling with Madonna.

Canseco knew that Major League Baseball was a business and owners needed celebrity sluggers to keep gate proceeds flowing in at a healthy rate. Old school managers could only discipline him so much. Yet the lack of a stringent demarcation between sports and show business is particularly disturbing for sports fans who love sports because they appear to be far from the institution of professional wrestling in which entertainment trumps all else. Sports fans love sports because presumably the outcome is not scripted like a movie or play. The worst nightmare of the NHL, NBA, MLB, and NFL commissioners would be if conspiracies of their leagues fixing games manifested themselves as truthful.

That being said, the close relationship between sports and entertainment has morphed into a cornerstone of American popular culture. The two lines of work have crisscrossed, intersected, and merged at every available juncture. When there has been room for the two industries to form a partnership, they more often than not have done so.

Music icons perform the National Anthem at the sporting world's most important events. For even diehard football fans, Super Bowl XXV was remembered as much for Whitney Houston's masterful rendition of the National Anthem as it was for Scott Norwood's botched game-winning field goal attempt at the final buzzer. In the midst of the Persian Gulf War, Houston's performance for the ages helped galvanize Americans in a patriotic ritual at a time when the country needed it most. Other entertainment icons such as Paul McCartney, Mick Jagger, Michael Jackson, Prince, Justin Timberlake, and Janet Jackson have all taken center stage during the halftime performance at America's most popular sporting event.

Pro basketball has formed a particularly cohesive bond with the entertainment industry. Sitting courtside at the Staples Center, Jack

Nicholson is a staple at Los Angeles Lakers home games. Post-season Laker games are often taken in by Adam Sandler, Steven Spielberg, Sylvester Stallone, Michael J. Fox, Charlize Theron, and Will Smith. Even before Kobe and Shaq, the great Los Angeles Lakers dynasty of the 1980's called itself Showtime. During the earlier rounds of the NBA Playoffs, the league's network station, TNT, airs commercials that jointly advertise the upcoming games with a soon to be released summer blockbuster movie.

Because elite athletes and performers are in the same income bracket, they naturally find themselves as neighbors in the same gaudy gated communities. Tom Brady's larger than life estate in Brentwood, California is just around the corner from actor Arnold Schwarzenegger's mansion. Nearby in Calabasas, former star wide receiver Keyshawn Johnson got into a well- publicized confrontation with entitled pop star Justin Bieber when the youngster recklessly drove his Ferrari around town.

And professionals in both fields often perform at the very same venue. The Beatles' last live performance took place on August 29, 1966 at San Francisco's Candlestick Park--the same stadium where Joe Montana starred for the San Francisco 49ers. One night Rihanna sits courtside next to the Brooklyn Nets' bench during a home playoff game at the Barclays Center. Twenty-four hours later she puts on a performance under the very same roof.

The marriage of sports and entertainment has also proven to be true literally as well as figuratively. Marilyn Monroe and Joe DiMaggio were the most famous couple in New York City in the 1950's. The pairing of Victoria and David Beckham is one of the relationships that international tabloids most closely monitor. Khloe Kardashian and Lamar Odom's marriage is one of the most iconic relationships in modern American culture. While they didn't marry, Derek Jeter and Mariah Carey had a fling in the late nineties when both were on top of their respective game.

Of course athletes such as Canseco represent one extreme, people with God-given athletic ability who have milked their craft for the sex appeal and entertainment buzz. Then there are former medical students turned pro baseball players such as brilliant and effective Red Sox relief pitcher Craig Breslow who gets to the clubhouse early to read the *New York Times* well before batting practice. Madonna and he may not be on each other's radar screens, but it's undeniable that at some level, a professional athlete playing in front of tens of thousands of people in person and hundreds of thousands on television can perceive himself as an entertainer. Both entertainers and athletes are not easily accessible to an enthusiastic fan base that pays good money to see them do what no one in the world does better. So it shouldn't be a surprise to see an athlete in a movie or television show, whether or not he is retired or active. Maybe what is really surprising is the fact that more athletes don't appear in movies and television shows.

Silver Sluggers on the Silver Screen

While Barry Bonds, Bobby Bonilla, and Pedro Guerrero did not have any spoken lines in the 1993 baseball comedy *Rookie of the Year*, all three sluggers were featured in the film's promotional trailer. During a summer in which the movie theaters were also bombarded with *Jurassic Park, Sleepless in Seattle, Free Willy,* and *The Fugitive*, the flick about a young boy pitching for the Chicago Cubs emerged as one of the most popular and highest grossing kids sports films of all time.

When the film was released in 1993, Bonds was not yet embroiled in the steroid scandal. He was fresh off his 1992 NL MVP season playing for a new team, the San Francisco Giants. He was the brightest star in a game that was not yet besmirched with labor stoppages and rampant Performance-Enhancing Drug usage. When sports fans heard that Bonds would appear in a movie, they flocked to the theaters. And Bonds, to his credit, was gracious about appearing in an iconic sports movie for younger audiences. The movie's star character was Henry Rowengartner, a 12-year-old Little Leaguer played by Thomas Ian Nicholas. Sports and Hollywood meshed as the superstar ballplayer went out of his way to embrace the up-and-coming young actor.

"We weren't expected to do that well. We were what you would call a sleeper hit, meaning that when the film kept climbing up in the box office everyone was just as surprised as I was," explained Nicholas, who has thrown out the first pitch at Wrigley Field during Theo Epstein's tenure as Club President. "They [Bonds, Bonilla, and Guerrero] were all really cool. At the time Barry Bonds was the biggest of the three and was ultimately the nicest of all three, not to say the others weren't nice. You would imagine that if someone grows in their prowess, that they would go in the other direction, but it was the very opposite."

Guerrero was retired when the film was released but Bonds and Bonilla were still two of the most feared sluggers in the National League.

"He [Bonds] actually stayed after he was done shooting his bit and watched me shoot a scene. We hung out for a little bit and I remember getting him to sign a baseball and he had written on it 'Barry Bonds--God Bless.' At the time I hadn't really signed any autographs and when the film started doing really well, I was signing pictures as well as baseballs and I remember paying homage to Barry. For the last 20 years I have been signing everything the same way. I kind of followed in suit."

For fans, watching fantasized cinematic depictions of their teams can be tantalizing. Pittsburgh Pirates' fans equate seeing Barry Bonds in Pittsburgh black and gold with the team's last run of success over 20 years ago. Chicago fans yearn for a real life Henry Rowengartner, a pitcher who can dominate opposing lineups and help the Cubs get their first World Series title since 1908. Many still wear the fictitious Rowengartner uniforms to Wrigley. And baseball fans across America gravitated towards *Rookie of the Year* because it was genuinely immersed in the country's hardball landscape. Whereas many other sports films use artificial stadium backdrops, *Rookie of the Year* was actually filmed at Chicago's historic Wrigley Field with live crowds. It was a fictional story encapsulated in the authentic setting of a cultural landmark. As there have been over a dozen new baseball stadiums constructed since 1993, the legend of Wrigley Field has only grown through the years. And the classic film set at the Friendly Confines remains etched in baseball and cinema history.

"The coolest thing for me was shooting on Wrigley on the field for a month. Obviously it's a bit different now and there are even fewer old stadiums left. At the time even then 20 years ago it was still one of three [old stadiums]. The Cubs have had their knocks and their downs so it kind of all coincides with that story. Cubs' fans aren't fair weather fans. They're in it regardless of what the Cubs have been through. So it's just kind of a special place."

Playing Cops and Pilots

Bubba Smith, one of America's most unheralded legendary athletes and actors, passed away in 2011 with an underwhelming amount of fanfare and attention. The behemoth defensive lineman who played for the Colts, Raiders, and Oilers made his first splash in the entertainment world with his trademark "easy opening can" line in Miller Lite commercials. He soon endeared himself to Hollywood with his charisma and articulateness. Shortly thereafter, Bubba Smith would become Moses Hightower, one of the legendary characters on the wildly popular movie *Police Academy*. The silver screen proved to be another arena in which Smith could flex his brawny muscles. The film portrayed him performing such herculean tasks as ripping the front seat out of a car and wrestling an alligator to save his friend's life. When the *Police Academy* series ran its course, Smith enjoyed smaller roles on such hit shows as *Charlie's Angels, Semi-Tough, Hart to Hart, Married with Children*, and *Family Matters*.

As a football player, Charles Aaron Bubba Smith played nine seasons in the NFL. In hindsight, one of the most ironic aspects of Smith's dual careers occurred during the 1969 Super Bowl. The New York Jets and Joe Namath defeated the heavily favored Baltimore Colts, a team anchored on defense by Smith. Namath may have gotten the best of Smith that day but over the course of their film careers, Smith had more cinema hits than Broadway Joe. As a television actor, Namath appeared on a wide variety of sitcoms, but his film career peaked with a spot on *C.C. and Company*. Meanwhile *Police Academy* became one of the most popular comedies of all time, spawning several sequels down the road. And Smith still won his football championship as the Colts defeated the Dallas Cowboys in Super Bowl V.

While it was ironic that Smith became more of a movie star than Namath, it was downright mindboggling that Kareem Abdul-Jabbar had a more vibrant cinematic presence than teammate Magic Johnson. As a player, Magic carried himself the same way that he does as a business tycoon and philanthropist. He is at ease mingling with the general populace--even when it is swarming him with hugs, autograph requests, and microphones. He embraces his rampant fandom with a seemingly genuine smile. As a center for the dynastic Los Angeles Lakers teams of the 1980's, Kareem was often dismissed as quiet and standoffish. Fans didn't always find him particularly charming and gracious. Unlike Magic, Abdul-Jabbar did not forge close friendships with Eddie Murphy and Arsenio Hall. Of all the great athletes of the late 1970's, Kareem the Dream seemed like an odd choice to drop funny lines in the 1980 comedy hit *Airplane!*

In one of the classic scenes, the boy roaming around the cockpit finally gets the pilot to actually admit that he is Kareem Abdul-Jabbar and not Roger Murdock. The movie was released in 1980 when Abdul-Jabbar was at the pinnacle of his basketball career so it only made sense for him to stay true to his basketball character. The comedic exchange went as follows:

"I think you're the greatest, but my dad says you don't work hard enough on defense. And he says lots of time you don't even run down the court. And that you don't really try except during the playoffs."

Kareem responds by saying: "The hell I don't. Listen kid, I've been hearing that crap ever ever since I was at UCLA. I'm out there busting my buns every night. Tell your old man to drag Bill Walton up and down the court for 48 minutes."

The world learned that one of the greatest centers in NBA history had a sense of humor. The entertainment world also learned that Abdul-Jabbar had a lot to offer to the industry. This wasn't Shaquille O'Neal starring in the film *Kazaam*. Abdul-Jabbar demonstrated his considerable cinematic talents by seamlessly blending into one of Hollywood's most iconic comedies.

When Abdul-Jabbar and his trademark skyhook left the NBA in 1989, he could have continued pursuing a career in the film and television industries. He could have let the *Airplane!* role be just a blip on the screen and eschew the publicity altogether. Like some other retired legends, he could have become more reclusive than J.D. Salinger and harder to find than Whitey Bulger.

To the surprise of many, the six-time MVP immersed himself in many different public arenas. He chose to have a cameo role in some of the most popular television shows of the 1990's including *Full House* and *The Fresh Prince of Bel-Air* while also serving as an assistant coach for the Lakers. He also has made celebrity guest appearances in the Macy's Thanksgiving Day Parade. But some of Abdul-Jabbar's most impressive contributions to American culture have manifested themselves in children's books. Perhaps his most unheralded contribution to the arts has been his recent spate of children books designed to enlighten youngsters about the richness of African-American history. Some of his best- selling titles include *What Color Is My World?* and *The Lost*

History of African-American Inventors. Despite recently battling Chronic Myeloid Leukemia, Kareem the Dream has toured the country to talk about his books and engage children in literacy projects. For Kareem, there is no better way to spend his elderly years than to enlighten younger Americans about cultural diversity and their ancestors' history.

Rhythm of Grace

The guitar is a fitting instrument for Bernie Williams. At the plate, the New York Yankees centerfielder was invariably calm and mellow. It didn't matter whether it was a Spring Training exhibition or Game 7 of the World Series. Bernie Baseball came across as the most relaxed person in the building. As an outfielder, he gracefully tracked down line drives soaring over 400 feet in Yankee Stadium's cavernous outfield. No one glided across the vast acreage with greater lithe and ease. A post-playing career full of sweet harmonic rhythms would be a fitting one for Williams.

"Rhythm and timing are all important elements of music, but they're important elements of sports. Especially baseball--you've got to have great timing to hit a baseball, you've got to have a sense of rhythm," explains Williams who has played everywhere in the tri-state region from the Stamford Center for the Arts to Madison Square Garden.

A bona fide five-tool player, Williams finished his spectacular career with a .297 batting average and four Gold Glove awards. Due in large part to capitalizing on many postseason appearances for the New York Yankees teams of the 1990's and early 2000's, Williams was considered a borderline Hall of Famer when he retired in 2006. Williams almost signed with the Red Sox in the days leading up to Thanksgiving Weekend 1998 but he did end up playing his entire 16-year career in the Bronx. The Red Sox were hoping Williams could replace the departing Mo Vaughn but instead the Yankees signed their beloved centerfielder before trading for Roger Clemens later that winter. As a native of Puerto Rico, Williams felt right at home playing baseball and later guitar in the Bronx. When he was a little boy growing up in Puerto Rico, Williams was mesmerized by baseball and his father's guitar playing.

On road trips, whether they were down I-95 or along the West Coast, the centerfielder would pack his guitar. He would serenade his teammates on plane and bus rides. Derek Jeter had a favorite falsetto for Bernie to perform. During one World Series victory parade through New York City, Williams played guitar music.

In retirement, Bernie, who now has a home in nearby Westchester, has found that guitar is a means for him to stay associated with the New York Yankees organization as he has played at Yankee Stadium before games. But he is also a popular musician not just because he is Bernie Williams, the former baseball star. In 2009 he was nominated for a Latin Grammy for his album "Moving Forward." Particularly in the summer months, Williams puts on smaller community based concerts in Connecticut and upstate New York. While the vast majority of Williams' shows take place in the Northeast, he hopes that his music will continue to serenade audiences across America in the coming years.

Those Who Try Reality Television

It is a good thing for the television industry that Y2K didn't wreak eternal havoc on Western Civilization. Since the dawn of the 21st century, the TV business has been buoyed by an industry wide revolution. The bonanza of reality and competition shows has forever changed the landscape of television programming. And athletes from many sports have been a part of the revolution.

One such athlete is Jeff Kent, a great baseball player who starred during the Steroid Era. During the time he played, no one spoke out more against steroid use than Kent. He played hard and he played hurt. Even more so than Bernie Williams, Kent deserves serious Hall of Fame consideration. He played in five All-Star games. On a San Francisco Giants team with Barry Bonds and Matt Williams, Kent was the MVP of not just his team, but the entire National League in 2000.

But few who were around Kent on a daily basis considered him to have a warm and friendly personality, the kind that would appear on one of America's most highly watched television shows. Early in his career, Kent publicly criticized former New York Mets teammate Fernando Vina when the two were competing for the starting job at second base. Later in his career, Kent got into a publicly televised spat with Bonds in the dugout. When he left baseball in 2008, he seemed like a prime candidate for a former player who would appear on television for the wrong reasons.

No one heard a peep from Kent for several years until 2012--and it turned out to be for a very fascinating reason. On the night of August 20, 2012, Kent became one of the most recognizable participants to ever grace the set of *Survivor*. Kent was introduced as a retired Major League Baseball player from Austin, Texas. He was one of the survivors competing for the one million dollar prize and title of Sole Survivor.

A reality show that called for grit and determination seemed ideal for Kent given his hard-nosed approach to baseball. Dodgers General Manager Ned Colletti, who served as an assistant G.M. for the Giants when Kent was on the team, knows that Kent was one of the true ironmen of baseball. "I saw him come into the clubhouse one day when we had a doubleheader and he was sick as could be, flu or something," said Colletti. "They hooked him up to an IV and he played the first game and we won. Between games, they hooked him up again, and he helped us win again."

A television role that called for mastering physical challenges was a good match for the former National League MVP. During this particular season titled "Survivor: Philippines," Kent expressed his new public identity to the world as he nestled in the backdrop of a breezy lagoon with his trademark mustache.

"I played baseball for 17 years. Now after retirement, I own a couple motorcycle dealerships. I have got a working ranch down south Texas. I have a second life. The opportunity that I think I have to win this game is because of the things that I have learned in baseball. People don't understand my competitive nature. They underestimate it. Throughout my whole life I have been a competitor. I am now a competitor in my second life. But I don't have my game face on like I used to. I am not so in your face. I am not so aggressive. When I played baseball in between the lines I was that way. I did everything I could do to win because I hated to lose. That is just my nature. I hate to lose. And that is what's intriguing to me about this game. It's not just challenges. I think you have to compete socially here. That's the social aspect of this game that's going to be the biggest challenge--dealing with people you don't like. In order to win, you're going to have to deal with people you don't like."

On television, Kent dished out the same brashly frank remarks he was notorious for in National League clubhouses. Players couldn't stand him unless they were wearing the same uniform--and even then that wasn't always the case. During an era in which guaranteed contracts leave some players more interested in taking days off than running out ground balls, Kemp's fiery zeal for competition never wavered. On television, he was the same Jeff Kent who terrorized National League pitching staffs. As long as he was getting paid to compete, there was nothing worse in the world than losing.

Other than Kent, relatively few baseball players have dabbled in television shows over the past several decades. The same cannot be said about football players and their affinity for the reality show known as *Dancing with the Stars*. The truth is that football players know dancing quite well. No sport more blatantly condones dancing as a means of celebrating success than football. On a more serious level, the nimbleness to elude an onrushing linebacker is akin to the footwork necessary for mastering various dance genres. For good reason, many of the stars on the hit television show such as Hines Ward, Donald Driver, Jerry Rice, and Emmitt Smith were former star employees of the NFL.

Soon after Smith, the NFL's all-time leading rusher, left football in 2004, he embarked on an entertainment career as a contestant on *Dancing with the Stars*. In fall 2006, Smith partnered with professional dancer Cheryl Burke to take home first place honors during the show's third season. The Smith/Burke duo actually finished the final round with the same exact point total as former *Saved by the Bell* star Mario Lopez and his partner, Karina Smirnoff. Ultimately, enough members of Smith's rampant fan base gave him the nod to win the tiebreaker. Smith was praised for "making dancing look manly" and for his "natural charm" while Burke was given kudos for coaching Smith yet still allowing him to improvise some moves.

Smith commented to the *Huffington Post* that: "It [being on *Dancing with the Stars*] opens another level of exposure I wouldn't get from the game itself. When I was playing the game, I had a helmet on my head; people rarely saw my face. I'm known as a champion on the football field, I wanted to be known as a champion in the ballroom. So you don't want to just get in for the exposure, because you can be exposed positively or negatively."

The man who spearheaded the Dallas Cowboys offense during the franchise's dynasty years has been busy in retirement. Smith pursued dancing competitions while he was embarking on commercial real estate ventures and broadcasting for both ESPN and the NFL Network. There was still room for dancing. After Smith spent years juking out defenders, impressing judges with swirls and shimmies proved to be another way he could demonstrate his unparalleled physical dexterity. Smith eventually returned to *Dancing with the Stars* for its all-star season. Just before Thanksgiving Day 2012, Smith was voted off the show along with fellow athlete Apolo Ohno in the semifinals round. For one of the rare times in his professional life, Smith experienced failure. As a football player who garnered multiple MVP awards and Super Bowl rings, Smith rarely absorbed the bitter taste of defeat. This time, as a celebrity dancer, Smith took the disappointment with his trademark good-naturedness.

"You can give your best, but sometimes your best might not be good enough. Somebody could do just that much better. But get back on the horse and ride it again, and have fun doing something else."

Since bowing out on DWTS, Smith has continued parlaying his charisma towards making the world a better place. While he is no longer a televised entertainer, his newfound company, Emmitt Smith Enterprises, has emerged as a global leader in real estate and charitable ventures. Still a young man in his mid-forties, Smith could very well find another avenue for re-entering the entertainment world later in life.

* * *

For retired athletes who can't get enough of performing for paying customers and television viewers, working in the entertainment industry is a dream come true. Similar to starting a career in broadcasting and business, entering the film, television, or music industry is infinitely easier when one already has the public fame and financial resources. Alas, entertainment can be more creative than broadcasting and less risky than business.

CHAPTER 6
Coaching: the Next Best Thing

The line between player and coach can be so blurry that often times the two positions cannot even be considered distinct entities. In this sense, the career paths of Bill Russell and Yogi Berra ran in parallel tracks as both legendary players assumed the hybrid position of player/coach for their respective teams during the late 1960's.

After the Boston Celtics won yet another world championship in the 1965-1966 season, Red Auerbach stepped down as Boston's head coach and passed the baton to Russell while he was still an active player. After the historic hire, Russell remarked, "I wasn't offered the job because I am a Negro, I was offered it because Red figured I could do it." As the first African-American coach in league history, Russell led the Celtics to a 60-21 regular season record in his inaugural coaching season.

Yogi Berra's transition from playing to coaching was not marked by a single and definitive demarcation. In June 1962, Berra, a grizzled veteran, remained behind the plate to catch a 22-inning marathon game against the Detroit Tigers. He was 37 at the time yet anecdotal evidence suggested he still had something left in his playing tank. After helping the Yankees get back to the World Series in 1963, Berra did call it quits as a player for the Yankees and assumed managerial duties for the Bronx Bombers the following season. When Berra's Yankees fell to the St. Louis Cardinals in Game 7 of the 1964 Fall Classic, Berra was out of a job.

Shortly thereafter Berra returned to playing (and coaching), for the crosstown Mets. In what many viewed as a slick PR move, the Mets let Berra play in four games while he was on the coaching staff during the early portion of the 1965 season. Albeit for a brief time, Berra did assume the hybrid role of player/coach en route to becoming a mainstay of the Mets coaching staff and ultimately taking over as manager in 1972 after the death of Gil Hodges.

The path Berra and Russell took towards coaching was fairly unconventional. Most players leave the game first and then pursue coaching. When they do so for their former teams, it is similar to a former student coming back and teaching at his or her high school. Sometimes it is hard to earn the respect of students who are of a similar age. For countless other reasons, coaching at any level takes a special type of individual who can both disseminate knowledge and relate to a diverse audience.

The Rare Basketball Coaches Who Played Professionally

On paper, it looked like a ridiculous mismatch. The 2004 NBA Finals pitted the Detroit Pistons against the Los Angeles Lakers--a team with four future Hall of Famers (Shaquille O'Neal, Kobe Bryant, Gary Payton, and Karl Malone) and one of the all-time great coaches in Phil Jackson. Meanwhile the Detroit Pistons team had one All-Star and not one player who was considered a lock for the NBA Hall of Fame in Springfield, Massachusetts. Yet the underdog Pistons inexplicably coasted to a 4-1 series victory over the Lakers.

For the Lakers, it was not quite a Hollywood ending to what was supposed to be a historic season. It was a break up the band type of summer with Shaq bolting to Miami, Payton to Boston, Malone retiring, and Kobe feuding with his coach.

Basketball junkies around the world were scratching their heads, wondering how a team with not one superstar could so easily defeat a star-studded Lakers squad. The 2003-2004 Detroit Pistons, a team coached by the estimable Larry Brown, are considered the epitome of what it means to be a team. In an age of inflated egos and hard to coach players, the Pistons coalesced into a collective whole in pursuit of a world championship. The following year a nearly identical Detroit team fell to the San Antonio Spurs in Game 7 of the NBA Finals. Similar to the championship teams Auerbach coached, not one of the Pistons was amongst the league's top scorers. Not surprisingly, alums of that historic Pistons squad have now parlayed their invaluable lessons and experiences towards mentoring modern hoopsters.

Corliss Williamson and Hubert Davis were not stars or even starters for that plucky 2004 Pistons squad. But they were trustworthy veterans who could provide a spark off the bench with their trademark grit and hustle. Williamson enjoyed a solid career in the NBA after emerging as one of the top collegiate players in the mid 1990's. Davis stretched out his career from 1992 when he was a rookie for the New York Knicks to 2004 when he was a back-up for Chauncey Billups.

Williamson and Davis are two of the most accomplished former players who have coached at the Division I level of college basketball. Professional basketball coaching staffs are rife with former playing stars. The college coaching landscape couldn't be more different. Many of the highly successful head coaches of the top programs such as Tom Izzo and Rick Pitino were not elite college players or professionals. Roy Williams couldn't even crack the varsity squad at North Carolina, the team he is now coaching. It is the same story in women's basketball. When Sheryl Swoopes was named the head coach at Loyola University Chicago in April 2013, she became the rare former WNBA star to coach at any level of women's college basketball.

In the mid-1990's, Corliss Williamson was synonymous with basketball in the state of Arkansas. There are no pro teams in Arkansas. Sports revolve around the University of Arkansas and Williamson, a native of Russellville, Arkansas, was emerging as one of the best basketball players to ever matriculate at the school. He led Arkansas to the 1994 national title game while being tabbed the SEC Player of the Year two consecutive years. After briefly exploring commercial real estate ventures upon retiring from the NBA, Williamson knew that his heart was set on the hardwood. He was willing to forgo a potentially lucrative business career for the sake of pursuing his beloved athletic craft. In 2010, he was named the head coach of Central Arkansas, a school in the Southland Conference that is located 30 miles outside of his alma mater. The school's claim to fame is that decades ago one of its student-athletes named Scottie Pippen served as basketball team manager before actually playing for the squad. Central Arkansas does not play against teams stacked with future NBA stars. It is a Division I school, but does not have the athletic prestige of a school such as Michigan State or Duke University. For many players on the Central Arkansas roster, this will be their last time playing basketball at such an elite level. Williamson believes in preparing his student-athletes for life after basketball as much as the game itself.

"Before retiring, I had coached my son's AAU team during my off-seasons. I enjoyed teaching the game of basketball. I wanted to share my experiences with other young men, so I started preparing myself for the transition about three years before I retired. After I fell in love with the game in the Fifth grade, all I ever wanted to do was centered around basketball. I knew before I ever thought about retiring that basketball would be a major part of my life forever. Through coaching I can still be competitive, and teach young men the life lessons I learned on and off the court. I believe the young men in our program respect the success that I experienced during my collegiate and professional career, but at times it is just like parents and their kids. They think times are different and we are being too tedious about how they are expected to play the game. If anything, I believe I am able to relate to them because it has not been too long ago that I was a player," said Williamson.

A first round draft choice of the Sacramento Kings, Williamson quickly emerged as an impact player. In only his third year in the NBA, Williamson was averaging nearly 20 points per night while guarding such megastars as Magic Johnson. He was the Sixth Man of the Year in 2002 and played alongside Chauncey Billups, Rasheed Wallace, and Richard Hamilton during many productive seasons in Detroit. As previously mentioned, the 2003-2004 squad was a selfless collection of professionals dedicated to a single goal. They were arguably not even the most talented team in their division, let alone the entire league. Larry Brown, now the head men's basketball coach at SMU, was able to milk every ounce of talent out of his scrappy Pistons team during the 2004 NBA playoffs.

"I was blessed to play under some of the greatest coaches in the game," added Williamson who played for Brown as well as Rick Carlisle and Rick Adelman. "I believe my latter years in the league when I was one of the "Vets" prepared me for coaching. After years of observing coaches and other veteran players during my early years, it was my time to help the younger players understand the game and what was expected of them. I really enjoyed that part of my career. I also miss the locker room, airplane, and bus rides! I loved playing the game at the highest level, but the fellowship with my teammates is the part I miss the most--the bonds and friendships that I will forever cherish."

While Williamson played basketball at the highest level of competition on the planet, he has the uncanny ability to personally relate to his understudies.

"A lot of guys who are good basketball players are not good basketball coaches because it came very easily for them," explained Nolan Richardson, who coached Williamson at the University of Arkansas. "Corliss is not that way. I really thought he would make a good coach."

And Williamson has done so at the Division I level of college hoops. At the end of the 2012-2013 season he decided to move on from being a head coach at a small school and become an assistant coach for his first NBA employer, the Sacramento Kings.

"I honestly couldn't see myself leaving for any situation other than an opportunity to go back to Sacramento. It's a place where I cut my teeth as a rookie in the NBA, spent over half of my career there. It's an area that reminds me a lot of Arkansas, with the people, the fans they have there."

In retirement, Hubert Davis returned to his collegiate alma mater by joining the University of North Carolina Tar Heels coaching staff after a successful stint in the ESPN broadcast booth. As an assistant for Roy Williams, one of the most successful and ethical head coaches in college basketball, Davis serves as a model of integrity and diligence. He was one of the few college standouts to not truncate his undergraduate studies for the sake of getting a head start in the NBA. By staying the entire four years at Chapel Hill, Davis not only graduated with a Degree in Criminal Justice but also played in 137 games while leading his Tar Heels to Atlantic Coast Conference tournament championships in 1989 and 1991. Davis poured in 1,615 points during his college years at Chapel Hill while cementing his legacy as one of the school's greatest long range shooters. Indeed, going back to coach at Chapel Hill was akin to a former student going back to teach at his or her cherished high school.

"I have loved this program since I was a little kid. My uncle Walter Davis played here from 1974 through 1977. I remember coming up here at four-years-old, watching him play. I had always wanted from a young age to go to college here and be part of a program," said Davis. "The opportunity to be able to play here and now come back and not only be a part of this program but raise my family here is just an unbelievable feeling. I loved this university and Chapel Hill my whole life. To have an opportunity to come back and work here has been absolutely awesome."

Davis spent his final playing days in the NBA manning the backcourt for the Larry Brown coached 2003-2004 Pistons team.

"I wish I could have played with Coach Brown earlier in my career. He cares about players, knows the game, loves teaching, and works hard. I really enjoyed the short time in Detroit playing for him, learning how he prepared, how he coaches, just how he prepares himself to put his team in a position to be successful. He is one of the greatest coaches of all time. Out of all the guys I played for, Pat Riley, Jeff Van Gundy, Larry was one of the greatest."

A decade earlier during the 1993-1994 season, Davis was a youngster on the veteran laden New York Knicks team led by center Patrick Ewing. During that particular season, Michael Jordan was on sabbatical, which allowed the Knicks to get past the Chicago Bulls en route to the NBA Finals. Davis and the Knicks fell to the Houston Rockets in an epic seven game championship series that occurred the same week in which the New York Rangers won their first Stanley Cup in 54 years and O.J. Simpson's Bronco chase took over the L.A. freeways and CNN airwaves.

Davis was one of several hoopsters to do the basketball trifecta: playing, broadcasting, and coaching. It seems like a popular career pattern for former backcourt veterans, as Doc Rivers and Mark Jackson have also served behind the bench and microphone after their playing days were over. At ESPN, Hubert was an analyst on the College Game Day shows leading up to big Saturday night games. His strong basketball acumen allowed him to appear on television screens in bars and restaurants across America on Saturday nights.

"I loved my time with ESPN and the part that I loved about it was the friendships that I made. I didn't work with Jay Bilas, Digger Phelps, or Rece Davis. Those guys were my friends. The part I really enjoyed was being around the coaches and players. The transition to here [UNC] wasn't a transition at all. I am able to do the things that I loved at ESPN but I get to do it in a more intimate way."

Backup Catchers and Utility Men Who Become Brilliant Baseball Managers

Few professions in life will allow the less talented employees to become the bosses of the more talented ones. In baseball, some of the most highly successful managers had limited playing experience at the big league (or minor league) level. The list includes amongst others: Terry Francona, Joe Girardi, Mike Scioscia, Ron Washington, Mike Matheny, Bob Melvin, Bruce Bochy, Eric Wedge, and Joe Maddon. Thousands of serviceable players pass through the ranks of the Major Leagues. Some enjoy a fairly seamless transition from player to manager while others don't even get an invitation to manage at the lowest levels of an organization. However in baseball, the progression from playing to coaching literally can happen overnight. A player retires and then becomes part of his organization's coaching staff. A shake-up in management occurs and before the retiree knows it, he is calling the shots, serving as the boss of guys whom he referred to as teammates merely a couple seasons ago. On October 14, 1996 Baltimore Ravens rookie linebacker Ray Lewis recorded his first NFL sack by corralling Indianapolis Colts quarterback Jim Harbaugh to the carpet of the RCA Dome. In the days leading up to the 2013 Super Bowl, Lewis was one of the players who Harbaugh was particularly concerned about in his pre-game preparation. National media outlets made the sack from 17 years ago into a storyline. In Major League Baseball, a manager competing against a former opposing player does not make for an attention grabbing story.

As a player, Eric Wedge lasted two and a half seasons, hitting .233 with five home runs. On October 29, 2002, Wedge was named the 39th manager of the Cleveland Indians. Over his first three years as manager, the Indians improved steadily. They finished in fourth place in the American League Central Division in 2003 before going 93–

69 and coming in second during the 2005 campaign. Wedge earned American League Manager of the Year honors in 2007 by leading the Indians to a 96–66 record en route to the franchise's first AL Central Division Title since 2001.

After the Boston Red Sox won multiple World Series titles in the early 21ˢᵗ century, the Tampa Bay Rays, under career minor leaguer Joe Maddon, emerged as the better team in the American League East. Although he won multiple Gold Glove Awards, Mike Matheny never knocked in 60 runs or hit higher than .261 in a single season. Yet as a manager, he led the Cardinals to the National League Championship Series in 2012 in his first season at the helm. Matheny was the successor to the legendary manager Tony La Russa, who as a player only hit for a .199 career batting average. Los Angeles Angels manager Mike Scioscia finished with a career batting average of .259 and never hit more than 12 home runs during a given season. As one of the longest tenured managers in Major League Baseball history, Scioscia directed the Angels to the playoffs in six of his first 10 seasons. Star players such as Vladimir Guerrero, Garrett Anderson, Josh Hamilton, Jered Weaver, Albert Pujols, Troy Glaus, and Tim Salmon have passed through the Angels clubhouse during Scioscia's tenure as manager. They checked their egos at the door and served as model employees for their boss.

Joe Girardi, who retired from playing in 2003 following a solid playing career, emerged as the perfect manager for the New York Yankees. Over the course of 15 seasons, he batted .267 and swatted 36 home runs. In his second career, Girardi is regarded as one of the game's best managers. He was named National League Manager of the Year in 2006 with the Florida Marlins and managed the Yankees during their 2009 championship season. Girardi's body of work is particularly impressive given the fact that he succeeded Joe Torre, a borderline Hall of Fame player himself, who managed the Yankees to four World Series titles.

In 2008, the new Joe had big shoes to fill. Torre could seamlessly handle the onrush of pesky reporters who swarmed into his office on a daily basis. When Torre became New York's manager in 1996, he quickly earned the respect of a roster that featured veterans Jimmy Key, David Cone, Bernie Williams, Tino Martinez, Wade Boggs, and Paul O'Neill. Girardi was another veteran player on this same Yankees squad that at the time included youngsters Derek Jeter, Andy Pettitte, and Mariano Rivera--all of whom would become some of the most iconic figures in the history of baseball. During the latter portion of their careers, Jeter, Pettitte, and Rivera have had to answer to Girardi. He also has had to manage a clubhouse of exorbitantly wealthy celebrity superstars such as Alex Rodriguez, Mark Teixeira, and C.C. Sabathia. During his first year as New York's skipper, the Yankees failed to make the postseason for the first time since 1994. Over the next several years Girardi would help the Yankees reemerge as one of the American League's top teams while cementing his place as one of the game's top managers.

Girardi knows that professional ball players like to be comfortable. It is incumbent upon the manager to make sure that such an aura of comfort permeates through the clubhouse and dugout. No sport has a stronger players union with such high salaried members. If a player is unhappy there are agents and social media for venting. Unlike professional football and hockey players, baseball players hold all the cards. Never in the history of the game has a baseball manager had to devote so much time and energy towards managing his players' personalities.

"As a player I knew that Joe would stay in the game. He is very intelligent to begin with, and has the ability to relate to players very well," said Scott Brosius, one of Girardi's former teammates in New York. "He is honestly a blend of Tony La Russa and Joe Torre in my mind. He is very prepared and detail oriented, hard-nosed and competitive. But he also has that same big picture perspective that allows him to relate to players at a personal level. He also has the courage to make tough decisions. He would be a guy I would love to coach next to someday."

Girardi was also known as a stand-up guy. As a player, he proved his leadership mettle not by catching a doubleheader in August or avoiding the Disabled List. On June 22, 2002, Girardi stood in the middle of the Wrigley Field diamond and fought back tears while he explained to a sold out crowd that there would be no baseball game today: one of his former teammates and best friends, Darryl Kile, had suddenly died of a heart attack in his hotel room.

In his second baseball career as a manager, Girardi has not wavered in his steadfast approach to handling matters both on and off the diamond. During Girardi's last season playing for the Yankees in 1999, he relished the opportunity to help mentor and train a young promising catcher named Jorge Posada. In 2011, Posada was in the waning days of his impressive career. Girardi knew it was in the best interest of the team to have Posada hit last in the batting order. When Posada balked at the assignment and subsequently elected to not play against the arch rival Boston Red Sox, Girardi didn't blink. It was batting ninth or not batting at all. He had no patience for prima donna behavior--even if one of his most loyal veterans felt betrayed.

Off the field, Girardi has done everything to uphold the dignity and maturity that come with having one of the world's most high octane and prominent coaching or managerial positions. On his way home from winning the clinching game of the 2009 World Series over the Philadelphia Phillies, Girardi stopped to help a woman who had spun out of control driving on the Cross County Parkway. Although the driver had crashed into the side of the highway barrier, she suffered only minor injuries, but Girardi felt inclined to make sure she received proper medical attention.

After winning their first World Series since 2000, the Yankees kept spending millions of dollars on top free agents. Some panned out while others did not. Some years have been more challenging than others. In 2012, the Yankees won 95 games and reached the American League Championship Series before getting swept by the Detroit Tigers. The following summer, the Yankees languished near the bottom of the American League East for most of the season as more than half their starting lineup was sidelined with injuries. To make matters worse, third baseman Alex Rodriguez was once again embroiled in a steroid related controversy. The Bronx may have been burning but Girardi remained as cool as ever during his most trying season as manager. Newly acquired veterans Vernon Wells, Travis Hafner, and Mark Reynolds were brought in while an assortment of freshly called up youngsters made contributions. Eventually many regulars returned from the Disabled List and the Yankees stayed in contention down the stretch. There was never a sign of panic from the man in the corner office.

"Joe's tremendous. Obviously given that he was a player, he understands injuries and what it takes to win. It's great to see him balance everything," said Yankees pitcher Joba Chamberlain, who has assumed many different pitching roles while playing for both Girardi and Torre.

When Girardi was a player for the Yankees, the Texas Rangers often stood in the way of getting to the Fall Classic. Over a decade and a half later, Texas is still one of New York's most feared opponents in the American League. However for the Rangers, the interim period was marked by a prolonged playoff drought. Their fortunes changed when Ron Washington, who had never managed at the big league level, took over before the 2007 season.

For a career, Ron Washington totaled 20 home runs and 146 RBI. Yet when he came aboard in Texas, he established himself as a players' manager who was particularly comfortable handling most high profile players. In his first year managing, Washington confidently stepped into a Rangers clubhouse filled with Texas-sized superstars, some of whom had even bigger egos.

"He had trouble earning the respect of Mark Teixeira, who viewed himself as a superstar--other guys, who viewed themselves as part of a team, no real problem. But, then again, Michael Young was helpful in that regard, urging him to be himself and be happier and more upbeat. That's what made Wash a well-liked player and a well-liked coach," commented Evan Grant, baseball writer for the *Dallas Morning News*. "I think when he came to the Rangers in 2007, in addition to having a team that was in transition, he also tried to act too much like a manager. He is who he is. He's not Buck Showalter or Joe Maddon. Once Washington got comfortable in his own skin - and the Rangers started to turn over the roster - both grew together at the same time."

By the time Washington came aboard in 2007, the Rangers were a perennially mediocre club. Some years they were cellar dwellers in the American League West. Long gone were the days of Rafael Palmeiro, Ivan Rodriguez, and Juan Gonzalez, stars who led the Rangers to multiple post-season berths in the late 1990's. Washington, who was portrayed as an Oakland A's infield coach in the movie *Moneyball*, was responsible for getting the Rangers back into the playoffs.

"Look at his record: this team improved in 2008 over 2007 and in 2009 over 2008. After Washington's first 50 games as Ranger manager, there was regular and consistent growth for both he and the team. Go back to the Teixeira trade - when everything changed for this team - and since then the Rangers have the fifth-best winning percentage in baseball. The teams ahead of them: Yankees, Phillies, Tampa Bay and Los Angeles. The only one of those teams to change managers was New York, from which Joe Torre 'resigned' following 2007. None of them have changed since. No reason for the Rangers to be any different. Washington matured and learned as a manager, got a stronger coaching staff and a better group of talent to work with," added Grant.

It got even better in 2010 and 2011 as the Rangers won consecutive American League Pennants. They lost to the San Francisco Giants and St. Louis Cardinals in the 2010 World Series and 2011 World Series respectively, but still established themselves as a legitimate contender in the American League West. For the first time in a long time, Texans spent some portion of their autumn evenings watching baseball instead of football.

"You know what you're going to get from him every single day. He's very consistent. He loves the game. He loves to teach it. He is very passionate about it. He's been the same way since the day I showed up here in 2007," noted David Murphy, a mainstay in the Rangers outfield who was acquired from the Boston Red Sox in exchange for closer Eric Gagne. "When you have a manager that preaches having fun and exemplifies that as much as he does it's easy as a player to show up to the park and not worry about the results but instead think about having fun every day, enjoying the game of baseball, enjoying your teammates. When it's that type of atmosphere, good things happen in the win column."

When Washington played in the 1970's and even 1980's, a Major League Baseball clubhouse looked very different from how it does in modern times. As baseball had only marginally tapped into the international pool of talent, there were very few Dominican players and virtually none from Japan. Now, Washington's best players (similar to those on most rosters) hail from far corners of the globe. Clubhouses have never been so diverse in the history of the game. When Japanese ace Yu Darvish first started getting acquainted with fellow Rangers players and coaches, he prioritized learning Spanish over English. There was more of a need to master the Latin American tongue. During Washington's playing days, Twitter was non-existent and multimillion dollar contracts were taboo. But the man affectionately known as "Wash" has a low key demeanor that gels with the vicissitudes of the modern-day game.

"He's gotten better every year. He got here in 2007 and he was never a manager before that. He's a very relaxed manager. He lets us do our thing. He says things that need to be said when they need to be said. He's very well respected," said Texas All-Star second baseman Ian Kinsler.

As a veteran ballplayer for the Minnesota Twins in the late 1980's, Washington was already honing his leadership skills as he mentored younger players, some of whom would go on to have long and successful careers in the Majors. For good reason, Washington's former teammates are not surprised that he is one of the most well regarded managers in the game.

"I remember Ron giving out advice. It came natural for him. Ron was very helpful in regards to the mental aspects of the game," recalls former Twins third baseman Gary Gaetti, who was a teammate of Washington's for several years. "He had a great personality, always upbeat and friendly. He was a great teammate. He had this calming effect because he had these experiences that he could tell you about, kind of give you some insight as to what to expect at different times."

Another one of Washington's teammates in Minnesota was Billy Beane, a hardball visionary and future General Manager of the Oakland Athletics. For over a decade, Beane's "money ball" philosophy has helped an Oakland franchise transcend financial limitations to remain competitive. Before becoming a manager, Washington was a valued member of Beane's coaching staff and was featured in the landmark *Moneyball* book and subsequent movie. In the book, author Michael Lewis wrote that "Washington was the infield coach because he had a gift for making players want to be better than they were--though he would never allow himself such a pretentious thought."

While the Rangers and Angels have become perennial favorites to win the American League West, the Athletics still remain a threat despite such stringent financial constraints. After a brief downturn, the Oakland franchise re-emerged as a particularly strong playoff contender when the easy-going Bob Melvin assumed managerial duties in 2011. It has been well publicized in books and film that Oakland is great at drafting and developing young talented players who eventually leave for opposing clubs. Melvin, a career .233 hitter, has overseen an A's team flourish with its eclectic roster of youngsters and reliable veterans. Thanks to an epic finish to the 2012 regular season, Oakland qualified for the playoffs while far more talented teams such as the Los Angeles Angels did not. The 2012 Angels had one of the deepest pitching staffs in baseball and one of the game's all-time greatest hitters in Albert Pujols. It defied logic, but the Angels finished five games back of an Oakland team that barely had any All-Stars.

Melvin's stint in Oakland was not the first time that he led a team of overachievers above and beyond expectations. In 2007, Melvin's Arizona Diamondbacks fell to the Colorado Rockies in the National League Championship Series. Outfielder Eric Byrnes led the Diamondbacks with 83 R.B.I. No starter hit .300 and other than Brandon Webb, the pitching staff was laden with journeymen hurlers. Somehow Arizona was one of the last four teams standing in the 2007 postseason.

"For me, playing for Bob was just real comfortable. He really let us play. When we didn't get off to a great start, there was no panic from his perspective. I think he really believed in us as an offensive team," said former Arizona infielder Craig Counsell, who used to play for Melvin.

Girardi, Washington, and Melvin may have played with very talented teammates but few have had such an indelible influence on America's pastime.

Baseball Lifers

The fans' most recent memories of a player are their strongest. They know even the heroes of the rinks, courts, and fields can only defy

Father Time for so long. Eventually, nature transcends the limitations of modern medicine and retirement beckons. At some point or another, there is an expiration date for a player. Blessed with God-given talent but still mortal, a 42-year-old can't do what he or she did at age 22.

But there is no such expiration date for a manager, which is why there are people like Jack McKeon who managed into his eighties. Some will go to great lengths to still patrol the dugout regardless of whether that dugout is in Fenway Park or on a small college field in the Pacific Northwest.

When he was still a relatively young man, Butch Hobson was manager of the Boston Red Sox during the 1992 and 1993 seasons. After the Red Sox sought a new manager following the 1993 season, Hobson moved on to become a minor league coach in the Philadelphia Phillies organization. Despite not getting another invitation to manage at the big league level, Hobson stayed in the game by becoming a manager in the Atlantic League, one of baseball's most well-known independent organizations. The league is a potpourri of career minor leaguers, journeymen MLB vets, and occasional former stars who can no longer perform in the Majors. Stadiums are located in small towns and typical crowds consist of several thousand fans. But it's still baseball and a way to make a living by playing a game.

"Baseball's all I've ever done since I left Alabama. I have been in independent ball since 2000. I can still manage and teach veteran guys who organizations have given up on," said Hobson, who was a third baseman for the Red Sox before becoming the team's manager.

"I grew up with a love for the game. I knew growing up with a dad who was a coach that I had some things I could offer as a coach or manager. I also like the farmer's attitude of giving a good hard day's work every day and I have always loved the outdoors."

Hobson may have devoted decades of his life to the baseball diamond, but he still remembers his days as a strong safety at the University of Alabama under head coach Bear Bryant. In college,

Hobson was a multi-sport athlete who competed against some of the country's most gifted football and baseball players during the fall and spring seasons respectively. He hasn't been involved in football since college, but the experience of playing for one of the greatest coaches in the history of collegiate athletics still bears an influence on his approach to mentoring younger athletes.

"I think the biggest thing I have had is a chance to play football for Coach Bear Bryant. We were prepared on Saturday. There was nothing left in regards to the preparation aspect of the game that we didn't cover during the week. He also taught us about life after football. We try to incorporate teaching life after baseball, whether it's becoming a coach or manager. Whatever it might be, hopefully we can teach them that."

Hobson had an impressive career, spending the majority of his time in Boston. While there were some defensive lapses in the hot corner, Hobson was a threat at the plate. He had his best year in 1977 when he drove in 112 runs for the Red Sox.

"I have always been able to be thankful that I got to play for the Red Sox, got time in the big leagues, something so many millions of young men couldn't do. I have had to accept the fact that I had my time. Now I teach, manage the game and give my team the best opportunity to win-- give them the opportunity that I had."

Before he became a long tenured manager in Independent League Baseball, Hobson was so highly sought after by the Red Sox to be their next manager that the team parted ways with local favorite Joe Morgan. When Hobson came aboard before the 1992 season the Red Sox hadn't won a World Series since 1918 and there was no such thing as Green Monster seats. A flapping Shawmut Bank sign and massive net hovered over the landmark left field wall. Sellouts and near sellouts were not the status quo. Larry Bird's retirement and Cam Neely's emergence into stardom relegated baseball to the backburner of New Englanders' attention despite the Red Sox having such stars as Roger Clemens, Andre Dawson, Mike Greenwell, Wade Boggs, and a young Mo Vaughn.

"It [managing the Red Sox] was easy when they are quality people like Roger and Andre. I had the utmost respect for the careers they had--so much greater than mine could have been."

As manager of the Lancaster Barnstormers, Hobson manages a roster that consists of some players who have never stepped on a big league diamond. College loans and off-season jobs are very much on their minds. Yet during the baseball season, they're still professionals and take losses hard. If they are not performing to their abilities, they can fall off the radar screens of Major League Baseball teams or potentially be released from their current Independent League team. Having played the game for decades, Hobson knows how frustrating it is to make an error or strike out--and how important it is to get over such mishaps quickly. When Hobson sees a player sulking after a miscue, he reminds him just how lucky he is to still be playing a kid's game in his adult years. He likes to tell his players, "I will give you my jersey. Just give me one more time to drive that runner from third in with less than two outs. I would change shirts with you."

Hobson continues to be known as a player friendly manager. He is used to weathering the baseball storms of losing streaks and extra inning losses. When Hobson occupied the manager's office on Yawkey Way, he penciled in Red Sox lineups that consisted of aging stars and undeveloped younger players. There were times in the season when Boston hovered around .500 before ultimately falling out of the pennant race by Labor Day after playing against American League teams featuring sluggers such as Frank Thomas, Mark McGwire, Ken Griffey Jr., and Joe Carter (a right-handed power hitter who always hit well at Fenway).

As a manager in Independent League Baseball, Hobson has enjoyed a more successful run. In 2012, his Barnstormers club established a new Atlantic League record by winning 88 games en route to reaching the Atlantic League Championship Series. Still, he knows that wacky and unpredictable events occur nightly on the baseball diamond. This is after all a sport in which the defense has the ball and failing the majority of the time while batting is analogous to success.

"If we have a bad night, I like to look it as I take the blame. You want your players to dwell on it for 10 or 15 minutes and then let the manager worry about it."

Hobson, who used to manage another independent club known as the Nashua Pride, has no immediate plans to leave the Atlantic League but would still explore other managerial positions if they were to become available.

"I could be the baseball coach at Alabama or anywhere in the SEC. I have got a lot to offer to college players. I believe in my heart I could win a national championship at Alabama."

Another former Major League third baseman, Gary Gaetti, manages in the Atlantic League. Gaetti was the rare professional ballplayer who played into his forties. As Gaetti played for multiple teams throughout the 1980's and 1990's, his offensive production numbers stayed at a high enough level that teams remained interested in his veteran services. He had a brief stint with the Red Sox in April 2000 before leaving the game as a player and later returning as a coach and manager. After serving on the Houston Astros coaching staff for a number of years, Gary became the manager of the Sugarland Skeeters, the only Atlantic League team not located on the East Coast.

"At that point [2000] I realized that the last couple years of being a former player, I really liked talking to the younger guys about a lot of the experiences I had in baseball. I tried to help and pass along some of the things that I learned. I guess at one point I thought about going into the ministry but I wasn't really qualified to do a whole lot else other than baseball. I like the teaching aspect [of coaching and managing]. That kind of comes naturally. Guys ask questions and need help and I've got a lot of those experiences where I can answer those questions and back it up."

For a good portion of the prior two decades, Gaetti was one of the most feared right-handed hitters in baseball. He was a two time All-Star who garnered four Gold Glove awards. A career marked by such longevity is going to coincide with many historical moments. In 1987 he anchored a Twins lineup that slugged its way to a World Series title. He was a teammate of Mark McGwire's during summer 1998 when McGwire shattered Roger Maris' single season home run record.

As third basemen, Hobson and Gaetti played at the hot corner of the diamond. For years they stood 90 feet away from right-handed hitters who whistled scorching line drives in their direction. Their careers have come full circle from where they started-- lengthy bus rides through vast expanses of rural America. And they are not the only ballplayers (or third basemen) to follow this career trajectory.

When he embarked on a managerial career, former New York Yankees third baseman Scott Brosius didn't return to the Minor Leagues but did go back to his alma mater, Linfield College. During his first six years as Linfield's manager, Brosius led the school to a 200-72 record and a Division III national championship in 2013. The vast and luscious backcountry greens of Oregon could not be more different from the bright lights of New York City. The breezes that cross the rolling hills of Oregon are calmer than the sometimes stuffy air that overhangs the Big Apple. The more laid back atmosphere inherent in managing a Division III school in the Pacific Northwest allows Brosius the opportunity to spend ample time with his family and stay involved in baseball. Like any baseball player, Brosius spent the majority of the year away from his family during his career. In his book *Last Night of the Yankees Dynasty*, Buster Olney wrote how Brosius was wrapping up his playing career for New York when 9/11 occurred. At the time, his three children had already returned to Oregon for the school year and his nine-year-old daughter Allison got on the phone to tell her dad "we need to be a family now."

"The balance was pretty important to me. That is why I was so excited about the opportunity to coach at Linfield," adds Brosius. "Staying in McMinnville allowed me to not move the family, and coaching at the Division III level allows me to be at home each night. My youngest is still in high school, and until he graduates I'd rather not upset our situation. I really didn't think about coaching until after my playing career. I think deep down I knew I would want to stay involved with baseball. I just didn't really know how that would look. My first couple years after I stopped playing - I don't use the word retired because I'm way too young for that! - I poured myself in to coaching my kids. I coached middle school basketball along with two baseball teams. I also helped out at the high school and Linfield. Over time, I was really drawn to the college side of coaching and my interest in being a head coach just developed over time."

Brosius, a consummate professional, embodied all that was great about the late 1990's Yankees teams that won multiple World Series titles. He was classy and clutch and endeared himself to fans across all five boroughs with his workmanlike attitude. In turn, the Yankees have welcomed his presence at ballpark events. He has been a participant in the annual Old-Timers' Day and his image still percolates through banners and plaque photos around the new Yankee Stadium. Before Game 6 of the 2009 World Series, Brosius threw out the first pitch. The starting pitchers that night were his former teammate Andy Pettitte and old adversary, Pedro Martinez. As previously mentioned, the Yankees went on to defeat the Phillies in the series clinching game.

Brosius turned out to be a fitting choice to throw out the first pitch. He had fond memories of October evenings in Yankee Stadium. During each of his first three seasons in pinstripes, the Yankees won a world championship. In 1998, Brosius capped off an All-Star season by earning World Series MVP honors as his Bronx Bombers swept the San Diego Padres in the 1998 Fall Classic. Perhaps Brosius' most iconic World Series feat occurred during a series that his team lost. The Yankees were down to their final out of Game 5 of the 2001 World Series, when he hit a majestic game-tying two-run homer that lit up the Bronx night and gave a city reeling from impossibly dark post-9/11 days a collective moment of relief. It was one of those times when sports provided Americans with a temporary escape from misery.

"I certainly miss the competition [of playing]. There will never be anything to duplicate playing in the World Series at Yankee Stadium! But I don't miss the travel and the time away from the family. I think regardless of how long you play you miss the games. I miss the clubhouse camaraderie, things like that as well. I miss being around the guys and competing together. You get some of that as a coach, but never at the same level as a player."

Having played in the MLB for over a decade, Brosius was around many hardball luminaries. For four seasons he occupied the left side of the Yankees infield with Derek Jeter. He played in dozens of American League games against Ken Griffey Jr. and Frank Thomas. And now as a manager himself, Brosius is able to emulate some of the game's most honorable managers who he had the opportunity to play for.

"I think I have drawn certain characteristics or aspects from each coach I have had over the years. Tony La Russa was the most detailed and prepared coach I had. Joe Torre was the best communicator and managed the personalities very well. He modeled a great life perspective, even in a place like New York City. Art Howe treated his players great and was a model of consistent professionalism. I think I have tried to bring those things that I appreciated about each of them into aspects of my coaching philosophy."

The High School Hockey Coach

To the casual observer, transitioning from professional sports to high school competition may seem like a letdown. But coaching is coaching. Even at the high school level, teaching others serves as the natural extension of playing. Coaching offers the stimulation of competition--a sensation that former athletes direly miss and cannot experience in broadcasting gigs.

Not every pro athlete wants to return to the podium, private jets, and daily scrutiny of managing world class athletes. There is a way to enjoy the game while not shouldering the burdens associated with professional coaching. There is a way to coach athletes who don't make hundreds of millions of dollars.

In 2010, three former standout Boston University hockey players, Tony Amonte, Scott Young, and Shawn McEachern, were named the head coaches at Thayer Academy, St. Mark's, and Rivers, respectively. After playing on Commonwealth Avenue in Boston around the same time, the trio of former Massachusetts hockey stars became rival coaches at the high school level in 2010. All three schools are members of the Independent School League (ISL), one of America's most prestigious prep school hockey leagues and breeding grounds for future pros. In the cutthroat world of hockey recruiting, these coaches, who had successful NHL careers after helping the BU hockey program flourish in the late 1980's and early 1990's, are able to leverage their pedigree towards attracting some of the region's top talent.

"Coaching just kind of came up. I got an email from St. Marks that they were looking for a coach. They asked with my connections and background if I knew of anyone. I was coaching my kids in youth hockey, and coaching was something in the back of my mind. I came out of retirement with the idea that something will come along. The legacy does help me. They do see my background," acknowledged Young, who netted over 300 goals and won two Stanley Cup championships in an illustrious 17-year NHL career. "I did get a lot of attention from families contacting me. Families and younger players do have a trust that I can help their kids develop. I took over a program [St. Marks] that was really struggling for three years. It is tough to recruit if the kids don't see an upside."

As it is in many cases, the coach benefits from the partnership just as much as his or her players do.

"As a player, after leaving that lifestyle, you can get bored. It doesn't matter about money, you're not getting that adrenaline rush, that high from playing, being out in front of the crowd," says Young, who happens to be coaching at his former high school. "You've got to fill your time. You can do golf trips with your buddies, but eventually you really need to find something to challenge yourself. It's important to stay busy. Although I didn't work right away, I was very busy running around with my kids. I lost a chance to see my kids play hockey and basketball all year and I wanted to be around my kids that first year away from the NHL. Now I do miss a fair amount of their games with the St. Mark's job."

Shortly after Young left Boston University to join the Hartford Whalers, the school welcomed aboard Tony Amonte, another gifted Right Wing who led the Terriers to the 1991 NCAA Division I Championship Game. Literally weeks after his final collegiate game, Amonte made his professional debut with the New York Rangers by skating in a couple games during New York's playoff run that spring.

Prior to winning the Stanley Cup in June 1994, the Rangers dealt Amonte to the Blackhawks in the middle of the season. For the rest of the nineties, Amonte would emerge as Chicago's best hockey player when the city's other indoor sport was dominated by Michael Jordan. During the final days of his borderline Hall of Fame career, Amonte played for a Calgary Flames team fresh off its 2004 Stanley Cup Finals appearance. And now, he is coaching players whose dream it is to follow in his footsteps.

"As a coach, I try to bring maybe not the NHL mentality but the mentality of striving to be good high school players, and using hockey to advance education. I have played with great leaders basically my whole career, guys like Mark Messier and Chris Chelios who know how to win. I have never considered myself a leader like that," said a guy who once served as the Chicago Blackhawks' captain. "I try to lead with actions over words. We try to instill leaders in our team. You don't have to say it, you do with it actions."

Before coaching Thayer's varsity team, Amonte actually helped coach kids in the middle school. When Amonte is not coaching other kids, he is a true hockey dad who wakes up before 6 a.m. on frosty Saturday mornings in January to warm up the car and head to Dunkin Donuts en route to the rink. Amonte also got his first taste of coaching by instructing his kids and then jumped at the opportunity when his former high school program called for his services.

"I started in the middle school, helping out with the younger kids. Was it [coaching] in the forefront of my mind? Not really. It's fun being around these kids. Coming from youth hockey, kids are a lot younger. High school kids tend to grasp concepts a little quicker. They're able to execute what you're telling them. The kids all want to learn, get better and go to the best schools possible. There's a lot of hockey up here, college hockey as well. Being back involved with the game is fun at whatever level whether it's scouting or coaching. I still love the game and I wanted to be involved somehow upon retirement."

Most of Amonte's players were babies when their coach was tallying over 70 points per season and representing America at the 2002 Winter Olympics in Salt Lake City. He will often show the Thayer players YouTube clips of his NHL playing days, some of which include the 1996-1997 season when he earned his first All-Star berth by leading the Blackhawks with 41 goals and 77 points.

"They get a good chuckle out of it. They do respect what I'm saying, where I came from. It is nice to be able to relate my experiences and let them know the mistakes I made and not to make the same ones."

Unlike Young and Amonte, McEachern had an inkling that he might want to be drawing up plays on clipboards after checking out of the NHL.

"Leaving the game hits you pretty quickly. I always thought about coaching. I finished up school online and I had been planning on getting into coaching. It's the second best way to stay in the game and feel the competitiveness of playing. When I was in Ottawa, Coach Jacques Martin said the best job in pro sports is to be the player. If you can't play, coaching is the second best option. He kind of told us that a lot," said McEachern.

During his rookie season in the NHL, McEachern won a Stanley Cup Championship with the Pittsburgh Penguins. He would go on to have some very productive seasons for the Ottawa Senators, Atlanta Thrashers, and Boston Bruins before leaving the rink as a player. Now in his forties, McEachern coaches young men who will be playing hockey well beyond their teenage years and others who will soon move onto other endeavors. But during practices and games, they are all dodging fore-checkers and sweating out grueling shifts before and after academic study sessions. There is no better coach to have than one who has succeeded as a student-athlete at both the high school and collegiate level.

"It helps that I've been in their situation. The stuff I have been through and seen, I realize it's a long process playing hockey for even a year. I feel very grateful to have made a living above and beyond whatever I expected to do. Playing hockey was something I dreamt about as a kid and I was fortunate to be able to do it for a long time."

Saved By Coaching

One would think that a guy who quarterbacked the Washington Huskies to multiple Rose Bowl berths in the early 1990's would be a high draft pick. The truth was that Mark Brunell didn't even come close to garnering the attention that Washington State's Drew Bledsoe and Notre Dame's Rick Mirer received from NFL coaches and executives leading up to the 1993 NFL Draft. Brunell had all the talent in the world but a devastating off-season knee injury spooked talent evaluators across the league from using their top picks on him. He would fall to the Green Bay Packers in the fifth round and appeared to be Brett Favre's backup for the foreseeable future. Then the Football Gods smiled on him.

There would be two expansion teams, the Carolina Panthers and Jacksonville Jaguars, joining the NFL at the beginning of the 1995 season. The Jaguars traded multiple draft picks for Brunell and subsequently tabbed him as the starting quarterback during their inaugural season. In only their second year of existence, the Jaguars reached the 1996 AFC Title Game where they nearly prevented Drew Bledsoe, Bill Parcells, and the rest of the New England Patriots from reaching the Super Bowl in New Orleans. For the next 15 plus years, Brunell would be named to three Pro Bowls, throw 23 touchdowns in the 2005 regular season, win a Super Bowl ring for the New Orleans Saints, and finish his career by serving as Mark Sanchez's backup in New York.

But Brunell's roller coaster ride of a retirement period makes his up-and-down NFL career seem like a kiddy ride. When Brunell left the NFL, he had liabilities of close to $25 million listed in his name and filed for protection under Chapter 11 of the U.S. Bankruptcy Court. While he was still playing football, Brunell made a series of poor investments in commercial real estate companies. For several months, the former NFL star made a living by serving as a medical sales representative while liquidating many of his personal assets including championship rings to pay off creditors.

Few could have predicted such trying times for one of the NFL's most respected players both on and off the field. When he played for the Jaguars, he was a staple of the Northern Florida community by establishing the Brunell Family Foundation that benefits critically ill children and their families. With a tireless work ethic, Brunell got the most out of every ounce of talent in his sturdy body to post career numbers of 32,072 passing yards and 184 touchdowns.

Similar to bouncing back from the aforementioned knee ailment, Brunell worked his way out of financial trouble to the point that he could return to doing something he loved for a living--being involved in football. Shortly after New Year's Day 2013, Brunell was back in the news for all the right reasons when the Episcopal School of Jacksonville hired him as the high school's new football coach.

"I've considered getting into coaching for quite some time. The concern I had about coaching on the college and professional level was the amount of time away from my family. High school coaching is family friendly and I have the opportunity to make a positive impact on my players. I did consider other careers, however being in football in some capacity was what I truly wanted to do. I enjoy the chance to make a difference in a young man's life. My role models growing up were my high school coaches. They were a very good influence in my life," said Brunell.

At any level, a football coach has to prepare his players for engaging in a physically grueling and violent contest. Brunell hopes to be the special leader who preaches the virtues of sportsmanship and moral propriety to young men who take everything he says to heart.

"I've been fortunate to have played for some very good coaches: Mike Holmgren, Tom Coughlin, Joe Gibbs, Rex Ryan and Sean Payton. I've learned so much from each of them. Each had his own coaching style and personality and was effective in their communication with their players. I guess what I really draw from as a coach was how smart and inspirational many of my coaches were. I would like to be that for my players. Not only teach them football but inspire them to be great people."

The bankruptcy situation may have been the most daunting Third and Long situation Brunell ever faced. Now that Brunell has moved on from that chapter in his life, generations of high school athletes will reap the benefits of learning from him.

Waiting in Line

Ironically, those with the most impressive playing resumes often have to wait the longest for head coaching gigs. Former utility players may seamlessly transition to successful coaching/managing careers, but many former stars struggle to land (or keep) head coaching jobs. To understand how success as a player does not translate to head coaching opportunities, one can look at Patrick Ewing. One of the NBA's all-time most revered and feared big men, Ewing tried to get hired as a head coach before he joined the Orlando Magic as an assistant. During that same time, one of Orlando's Eastern Conference rivals, the New Jersey Nets, were led by diminutive Lawrence Frank, a long tenured NBA coach who was unable to make his high school basketball team. In college, Frank was the manager of the Indiana Hoosiers. When he was at Georgetown University, Ewing was one of the top players in the country. After his time in Orlando came to a close, there was scant interest around the league for Ewing's coaching services. Finally the Charlotte Bobcats hired Ewing as an assistant coach prior to the 2013-2014 season.

"First of all Patrick Ewing is the best superstar I ever played with," exclaims Hubert Davis, who was a former teammate of Ewing's in New York. "He is one of the best players in NBA history. I came in as a rookie and I played four years with him. The way he communicated and made me feel part of a team--I couldn't ask for anyone better. He was the best leader, the best teammate, and those are the types of qualities that make him a great coach."

Robert Parish, another all-time great center, has had trouble joining any coaching staff while battling personal and financial issues away from the game. As Parish has found out the hard way, being named one of the 50 Greatest Players in NBA history doesn't guarantee him an invitation to coach, especially when he has been away from the game so long.

"I'm ready to do something. I want more on my plate. I want to be busier. I take most of the blame because when I retired, I basically disappeared," Parish told the *Boston Globe*. "I didn't want to do anything for a long time. And when I played, I didn't foster any relationships that could benefit me now. I kind of did my own thing. A lot of this, I bring on myself. I feel like, had I reached out to people when I first retired, I think it would've been a lot easier to get work as opposed to 16 years later."

Ryne Sandberg, one of the most skilled second basemen of the late 1900's, received the ultimate athletic accolade by being inducted into the Hall of Fame in 2005. In the heart of the steroid era, Sandberg's Hall of Fame credentials were boosted by a presumably clean image. Still his career numbers were nothing short of impressive: 2,386 hits and 344 steals. After 16 storied Major League seasons, Sandberg would have to start all over again in the Minors to launch a new career as a manager. He had to put in his dues again by enduring endlessly long Minor League bus rides for years before the Philadelphia Phillies hired him as a third base coach and eventually promoted him to manager at the end of the 2013 season.

Washington Capitals head coach Adam Oates also knows that the coaching profession is not immune from the "patience can be rewarded" cliché. As a player, nothing came quickly or easily for him. During the first chance he had to get drafted, every NHL team passed up on him. He moved on quickly, enrolling at Rensselaer Polytechnic Institute (RPI) before having a spectacular college career. After graduation, Oates signed a lucrative rookie contract with the Detroit Red Wings.

"I was kind of a late bloomer," said Oates. "When the scouts look at the draft, they look at the big kids. I was a small kid that slipped through the cracks. It allowed me to go to college, and then came that second wave of guys that got signed. Growing up, I was a guy who was kind of overlooked and I was fortunate to have the opportunity to go to RPI and have the time for my game to mature."

Oates established himself as one of the game's elite playmakers over the course of his Hall of Fame career. The 19-year veteran who totaled over 1,000 assists coached at the minor league level for the New Jersey Devils and Tampa Bay Lightning organizations before becoming Washington's head coach prior to the 2012-2013 season.

"Yes, Wayne Gretzky was the best player to ever play the game, but I'll tell you one thing--in my era it was Wayne and Adam Oates for playmaking," said fellow Hall of Fame inductee Joe Sakic. "He made everybody around him better. If there is a guy you want on your team to set anybody up, it was Adam Oates. He was unbelievable--one of the best playmakers of all time."

Oates' cell phone had a busy day on June 26, 2012. On the day Oates was notified of his induction into the Hockey Hall of Fame, he received word that he would be Washington's new head coach.

In his new position, Adam would be coaching one of the several teams that he starred for as a player. Even in the NHL, few head coaches were superstars as players. Now, the former Boston Bruins center had the advantage of being able to relate to Alex Ovechkin and Nicklas Backstrom, the young megastars who comprised the core of his team.

"It's always easier to relate to somebody who has been through it and someone who knows what it's like not just as coach but as a player. He's a great guy to learn from, one of the best. He's somebody who not only knows the game so well and has been so successful in the game but he's so passionate about the game. That's a valuable tool for any hockey player to have a guy like him teaching us. It's huge to have a relationship like that with a coach," said Backstrom.

Part of the reason it took Oates nearly a decade to find a head coaching vacancy was that he elected to put hockey on ice for the sake of spending more time with his family and friends.

"Sometimes it's tough when you quit playing, it's such a large part of everybody's life that plays the game. It's hard to jump right back into things. Obviously coaching and playing are a lot different. Sometimes it's tough to get behind the bench when you can only do so much. You can't be out there with the guys battling and doing what you can to help the team win," added Backstrom.

As a first year head coach in Washington during the lockout shortened 2013 season, Oates coached a Capitals team that struggled to coalesce after many players went overseas during the extended off-season. They didn't get off to the greatest start but management stuck with Oates behind the bench, believing his levelheadedness and hockey acumen could eventually pay dividends. In the second half of the season, the Caps roared back to make the playoffs and nearly upset the New York Rangers in the opening round. The Capitals are committed to Oates, as they believe he can lead the team to a Stanley Cup Championship before the Alex Ovechkin Era in D.C. winds down.

"When I retired I guess I felt it was time to take a break from the game. I had been in it a long time," acknowledged Oates. "I didn't realize how much time is actually involved in it. You spend a lot of time at the rink and it's amazing how much time the coaches think about every little decision and how much you interact with each other and the commitment to the players. I never envisioned that as a player it was that much."

Small School Athletic Directors

There are smaller towns than Plymouth, Wisconsin and Fairfield, Connecticut but neither outpost will ever be considered a viable stage for big time athletics. Nestled on the banks of Lake Michigan just north of Milwaukee, Plymouth is home to Lakeland College, a Division III school belonging to the Northern Athletics Conference. The town of Fairfield is a college town home to Sacred Heart and Fairfield University and happens to be sandwiched between Bridgeport and Stamford along I-95. It is an hour train ride away from Grand Central Station. Interestingly, the athletic departments of Lakeland and Sacred Heart have been spearheaded by Athletic Directors who behold celebrity and legendary status in the sporting community.

Kellen Winslow, a 1995 Hall of Fame inductee and arguably the best tight end to ever play in the NFL, had to Google "Plymouth, Wisconsin" to see where exactly he would be going for the interview for the school's AD position. The school's new president, Michael Grandillo, had known Winslow for years and believed there was no better role model for his community of student-athletes. At Lakeland, there are fewer than 1,000 students, and most play on one of the school's 18 athletic teams.

Over a quarter century removed from his last NFL snap, Winslow opted to stay involved with athletics for the sixth consecutive decade of his life. In his mind, the world of sports serves as a galvanizing force for Americans, providing them with a critical vehicle for forging a collective identity.

"In 1980, when the United States hockey team won the gold medal at the Winter Olympics, I knew very little about hockey but I was sitting in front of that television cheering 'USA'! In 1936, when Jesse Owens dominated the Summer Olympics, Jesse Owens was not a man of color. He was an American. And we all got behind that. And that's the power of athletics."

In a bizarre coincidence, the greatest athlete to come out of Lakeland College is Pat Curran, the former San Diego Chargers tight end who Winslow replaced when the bolts drafted him in 1979. Winslow knows that Curran is an anomaly for a Division 3 athlete. The overwhelming majority of student-athletes at Lakeland need to prepare for other professions upon graduating. As an AD, Winslow believes it is incumbent upon him to oversee a 100 percent graduation rate amongst student athletes.

"It's all about the students. I told my coaches these are my kids. I take that very seriously. You are responsible for my kids and anything less than a 100% graduation rate is not acceptable," explains Winslow, who served as Athletic Director of Central State University before taking the same post at Lakeland.

Halfway across the country, another former athletic standout assumed the AD position for a school in which athletics takes a backseat to many other matters. After successfully managing the Chiba Lotte Marines in Japan, Bobby Valentine tried to resurrect his Major League managerial career with the Boston Red Sox during the 2012 season. It was a train wreck from Day One. His star players called him out in the media while fans were calling for his head. By Father's Day, the consensus was that Valentine had lost the clubhouse. After leading the Red Sox to a 69-93 record, their worst in years, Valentine was fired on October 4, 2012.

At 64-years-old, Valentine could have easily retreated to his chic Stamford restaurant or busied himself with gardening and painting. But athletics stayed in his blood. The opportunity to impart his wisdom and experience on young athletes without the politics inherent in the professional ranks was too enticing. Shortly after Boston fired Valentine, Sacred Heart hired him as the school's new Athletic Director.

"At this juncture of my life I feel I'm in the middle of my life. I'm a guy who loves to do things, a guy who loves challenges. I opened up a restaurant in 1980 and never flipped a hamburger before. I do things that are presented to me so that I can be challenged. I have lived in five different countries, and I have spoken different languages," said Valentine.

At Sacred Heart, there would not be the stimulation of competing against Derek Jeter in a packed Yankee Stadium on ESPN Sunday Night

Baseball or calling games on the weekly broadcast (something he excelled at for several years). But as Valentine approaches his elderly years, the AD position allows him to continue having an influence on athletics. Despite his colossal failure as Red Sox manager in the 2012 season, no one could take away from Valentine the fact that he enjoyed a decade long career in the Major Leagues, which came on the heels of being courted by Division 1 football programs. He is pursuing a noble course of action: leveraging his prior experiences and successes towards having a positive influence on student- athletes in his neighborhood.

"I'm hoping that the things I have touched in the past and the associations I have made and the people that I know can facilitate everything we might try to do here, whether it's fundraise or win a baseball game," says Bobby V, who often rides his bicycle to work from his Stamford home.

Bobby V's fingerprints are all over Southern Connecticut. His new AD role and popular Bobby V's sports bar make him one of the most prominent athletic figures in Connecticut, not far behind Geno Auriemma and Jim Calhoun. Few athletes and coaches enjoy such a wealth of diverse experiences around the globe and then return to focus exclusively on their home region. For Valentine, an ambitious and personal man who can't get enough of the spotlight, Sacred Heart is a perfect fit. The school is small enough for Valentine to become immersed in the campus but still big enough for him to remain an influential figure in the Division 1 college athletics landscape.

* * *

For many, going from playing to coaching is the most natural career progression in the world. But not everyone can do it. Tino Martinez, a phenomenal Major League hitter, was an abject failure during his brief stint as hitting coach for the Miami Marlins. Under his watch,

Miami was the worst offensive team in baseball. When enough players complained of Martinez's over aggressive tendencies that bordered on verbal abuse, he had to find something else to do in retirement. When they got their chance, retired legendary players such as Dave Cowens, Willis Reed, Bart Starr, Ted Williams, Jimmy Connors, and Wayne Gretzky didn't last long as coaches or managers. As the hackneyed expression goes, sometimes the best players don't necessarily make the best coaches. It can get frustrating trying to teach others a skill that comes so easily to oneself. Sometimes, it's hard to explain who or what makes the best coach, which is why the great ones should be appreciated.

CHAPTER 7
Practicing Sports and Law

"He has excelled at everything. And I know that he will excel on the highest court in the land."

President John F. Kennedy heaped such praise on Byron White upon appointing him to the Supreme Court in 1962. When JFK made the comment about his new Supreme Court appointee, he must have been bearing in mind White's exploits on the football field.

Before he underwent the fourth longest Supreme Court tenure in the history of 20th century America, White emerged as an All-American running back at the University of Colorado and the leading NFL rusher during the 1938 and 1940 seasons. A member of the 1940's NFL All-Decade Team, White enjoyed a highly successful NFL career when the league was still in its nascent stages. Soon after fulfilling his naval duties in World War II, White left football to embark on his full-time legal career.

Byron went on to earn his J.D. at Yale Law School before becoming a Rhodes Scholar recipient and later U.S. Deputy Attorney General. As a Supreme Court justice, White ruled on such landmark cases as *Roe v. Wade* and *Miranda v. Arizona*. In 1993 Vice President-Elect Al Gore asked for White to administer his oath of office to become the 45th United States Vice President. When White passed away in 2002, his feats as a running back were a mere footnote to his profound influence on America's legal system.

Ron Mix, Mel Owens, Alan Page, and Dave Shand are several former gifted athletes who had the foresight and maturity to realize that even if their professional athletic careers did materialize, there were still many years to live afterwards. Enduring grueling workouts by day and studying for the bar at night is not the easiest way for one to spend his twenties. But their ability to sustain successful careers demonstrates how entering the legal profession can be a viable means for a retiring athlete to segue into another realm of professional life.

Nevertheless, this chapter still represents the most succinct segment of the entire book--or for that matter nearly any account of former professional athletes. One could almost count the number of former pro athletes who have transitioned to a legal career upon retiring from athletics. From a pragmatic standpoint, it makes sense. Leveraging one's star power towards establishing an entertainment or real estate business is a little more appealing and easier than pursuing a law degree. Being the face of a successful restaurant is often perceived as the definition of fun. Endorsement deals and broadcasting gigs are cushy. But there is nothing fun or cushy about studying for the LSATs, going to law school on a full time basis for three years, studying for the bar, passing the bar, and starting a practice while still nursing lingering ailments from playing days. Many former pro athletes have the intellectual curiosity and activist spirit, but understandably there is often less incentive to embark on such a rigorous line of work when opportunities abound for opening up a chic night club in a bustling downtown area. However, for some former athletes there has been and always will be an incentive to practice the law.

Helping Former Gridiron Brethren

It is rather ironic that football players, some of the world's most powerful and wealthiest individuals, can become so vulnerable and in dire need of outside assistance upon departing from their sport. The aforementioned accounts detail the successes, riches, and joys of athletes who have prospered in retirement. Yet the inconvenient truth is that legions of former pro athletes suffer from emotional, financial, and physical burdens. And for the most part, their stories go unnoticed. For every well publicized Antoine Walker tale, there are hundreds of ex-athletes struggling from chronic injuries in relative anonymity. And no professional league is burdened by more former participants suffering from health related issues than the NFL.

As a collective whole, former pro football players have started to emerge to the forefront of the public's attention. For players who were in the league before the 1990's, there was scarce attention paid to the prevention of concussions--one of the chief maladies that plagues ex-NFL players. Some former NFL players need protection and attention to get back on their feet and function with some level of competency in their re-entry to the real world. There has been exemplary work done in the private sector to alleviate the suffering. Mike Ditka's Gridiron Greats Assistance Fund is one such notable program. Yet some former footballers turned lawyers realize there is room for helping out their fellow tormented brethren.

One ex-jock turned attorney, NFL Hall of Famer and former San Diego Chargers standout Ron Mix, has devoted his practice towards helping fellow members of the football brotherhood obtain their well-deserved compensation packages long after they have retired. Since the early 2000's, representing professional athletes in filing such claims has been his full- time job. Prior to such work, Mix spent several decades working as a civil court litigator. Ultimately, he found a vehicle for leveraging his legal expertise towards assisting some of the most desperate and neglected members of the 20th century workforce.

"In my current practice, it is gratifying to assist former fellow athletes because the benefits I obtain for them often come at a time when they need it most. Most clients receive tax-free cash awards in the $100,000 plus range. For many of my clients, this becomes a second chance at financial stability. As is well known, post-careers have most often been unkind to professional athletes," says Mix, who was known in his day as the Intellectual Assassin for his sharp mental acuity that complemented his physical litheness. In his elder years, he has profound insight into how former athletes can put themselves in the best situation to flourish after the final whistle.

"One way to prepare emotionally is to understand that only a small percentage of the adult life will be spent as a professional athlete so expose yourself to a wide variety of other interests, including continuing your education. Do not become involved in businesses during your playing career; every business requires complete attention; be conservative in your spending and investments; even to the extent of placing a certain percentage of your earnings into annuities that provide guaranteed, creditor-free, income in retirement.

"How to prepare physically: (1) continue to exercise; (2) if you played a position that had the job requirement of being overweight (linemen in football), lose weight upon retirement; (3) you made a ton of money; spend some of it on health and nutrition consultants and personal trainers: (4) if you played a contact sport (that means most sports), have complete neurological and medical examinations on a regular basis, including during your playing career. Brain damage is real. It should be monitored."

No generation of retired football players has been exempt from the unkindness that Mix references. For NFL players from the 1960's, 1970's, and 1980's, an early career ending injury often served as the massive boulder that Sisyphus had to roll interminably up and down a hill. A lack of long-term care benefits, overemphasis on one facet of life (football), and modest income served as a perfect concoction for misery and helplessness. Each story sounds worse than the one before. Andre Waters, a star safety for the Philadelphia Eagles and the Arizona Cardinals, committed suicide at the age of 44. He was suffering from brain damage caused by multiple concussions during his 12-year career, according to pathology reports. After 12 years as an NFL defensive lineman, Mike Pitts has dealt with memory loss, fatigue, mood swings, and headaches. Former New England Patriots fullback Kevin Turner has struggled financially while battling ALS. Many people wonder if Turner's terminal illness at least partially stems from a spate of football related concussions.

In another sense however, it was easier for NFL players a half century ago to prepare for retirement. Whether they played two or 22 years, the aggregate compensation amount could not provide financial comfort. Thinking about other careers was a means of survival. Times have changed. Lured by gaudy signing bonuses and enticing contract options, today's gridiron greats often lose sight of the fact that when they suffer grave injuries, their contracts can become null and void in a heartbeat. A contract that had seemingly beheld financial security becomes an empty promise.

But it doesn't need to be that way. Modern NFL players who stay in the league for several years do have significant income and resources to counter health issues that are inevitable from playing one of the most grueling and taxing sports in the history of humankind. Mix hopes that the modern players don't have a myopic mindset in regards to their current and future career options.

"I played between the years 1960 through 1972," explains Mix. "At the time I played, the earnings were so modest that most players knew that they would not leave the game independently wealthy no matter how long they played. So they began preparing for their exit from the game right away by continuing their education or working at jobs during the off-seasons. I went to law school part-time for four years, during the football season and during the off-season. The modern players make so much money that they do not have to prepare for a second occupation....at least that is what they think. The naked truth is that most professional athletes come from similar socio-economic backgrounds, growing up poor without any business sophistication in the family and the circle of friends. Because they were poor, they are too sympathetic and too generous with their money to family and friends. Because they are not sophisticated, they are easily duped into high-risk investments. Once their careers are over, 99% do not have any marketable skills. Playing sports in college takes up so much time and energy so most players leave college without truly receiving a college education. Even if they did, by the time they are ready to enter the market, they are already, depending on the length of their professional careers, 5 to 12 years behind their former college classmates."

In modern times, many pro athletes have even been discouraged from fulfilling requirements for completing their undergraduate degrees. In the months leading up to the 2011 NFL season, former New England Patriots defensive end Ty Warren forfeited a $250,000 off-season workout bonus so he could obtain his degree in Agricultural Leadership and Development from his alma mater, Texas A&M. Warren wanted to be the first one in his family to graduate from college and thus he made a pledge to his relatives that he would receive the diploma. Nevertheless, Warren did hear whispers on sports talk radio that as a well paid employee of the New England Patriots, he should have been exerting his efforts on the training fields and not in the classroom.

In May 2001, NBA All-Star Vince Carter spent the morning of Game 7 of the Eastern Conference Finals flying down to the University of North Carolina to get his undergraduate degree at the school's graduation. Carter left UNC after his sophomore season to enter the NBA Draft but continued to take courses during the off-seasons of his budding career. On the morning of the Toronto Raptors' biggest game in franchise history, Carter was trying to make good on his promise to his mom rather than worry about the opposing Philadelphia 76ers' defensive schemes. Ridiculously, Carter also received some amount of criticism for pursuing one of life's most noble achievements, a degree in higher education. Carter's coach, Lenny Wilkens, warned him that he would be exposing himself to severe criticism if he didn't perform well in Game 7. He did perform well, finishing with 20 points and nine assists. Most importantly, he showed that family can be the greatest motivator when it comes to pursuing education.

Carter's successful completion of an undergraduate degree is a relative anomaly in the world of professional athletics. Many top collegiate football and basketball players eschew the latter part of their college careers to ink their first pro contract. Many pro baseball and hockey players get drafted out of high school and skip college altogether. This sad reality has been true for years even when the makeups of the leagues, and particularly the NFL, have changed drastically. When Mix played in the 1960's and 1970's, the landscape of the NFL was very different from what it is today. Concussion awareness programs were taboo. Players made modest salaries. Pro football was not the multi-billion dollar enterprise that is the National Football League at this hour. However, under progressive minded commissioner Roger Goodell, the NFL has made great strides in promoting issues of health awareness and helping players prepare for post-playing challenges.

But such challenges remain, due in no small part to the NFL owners' unwillingness to provide greater benefit packages to retirees. The NFL's Disability Board, run by league management and the Players' Association, rejects almost 60 percent of the claims it sees. Many feel it is unjust that billionaire owners even debate how long they should be responsible for footing healthcare bills for the men whose trials and tribulations generated such profiteering. For football players who played at least four years, the NFL does provide health insurance for up to five years after retirement. Many pundits think the league gets off easy here given that the vast majority of injuries such as hip replacements and neurological defects are long-term issues that necessitate treatment after the aforementioned window of time.

The New England Patriots beat writer for the *Boston Globe*, Shalise Manza Young, noted that, "It is true that players signed up for an NFL career of their own volition, and there are risks involved. But when the league insurance runs out after five years, what then? Few, if any, companies will insure individuals with a preexisting condition, or if they do, the premium is astronomical. There is no denying that players today do earn a good salary. The minimum for rookies in 2013 is $405,000, and the league-wide average is $1.9 million. But the average salary was $90,000 in 1982. The cost of care that players from that generation now need far exceeds that. Should the NFL be responsible to those men? It is not as if the league will feel the pinch — the NFL pulls in $9.5 billion in revenues annually, and all 32 teams are among *Forbes* magazine's 50 most valuable sports franchises in the world. The profits they enjoy now largely came on the backs of those men, who helped popularize this brutal sport and make it into the entity it is. For many of those men, even standing up for any length of time is painful, and sadder still, some may not be able to remember those glory days if a neurocognitive condition sets in."

Irrespective of inflation and poor money handling decisions, the discrepancy in salaries between the generations of players is egregiously disparate. Yet many of the more recently retired players are well aware of their predecessors' predicament.

"You really want the retired players to get better healthcare, better pensions," former Green Bay Packers wide receiver Desmond Howard acknowledged. "These are the people who paved the way for the younger guys who are playing and actually benefiting from what the older guys accomplished."

And that is why attorneys such as Mix who have dedicated their professional lives towards helping neglected athletes are so indispensable.

Mix's work ethic in the trenches of the gridiron would foreshadow his relentless pursuit of justice as an attorney. When he was an offensive lineman, Mix did much of the dirty work at the line of scrimmage. Mix is to the San Diego Chargers franchise what fellow Hall of Fame lineman John Hannah is to the New England Patriots. Mix may not be the most ballyhooed star in the league's history but he was just as influential as any of his fellow Hall of Famers. To the extent that an offensive lineman can receive recognition, Mix did so. After Mix's Chargers won the 1961 AFL Championship Game, *Newsweek* commented that "Mix is not only the best offensive lineman in the AFL; he is also a performer with enough dash to draw one eye of the spectator away from the glamour of the backfield." Even the most seasoned football experts focus the majority of their attention on following the ball. To make a visible impact away from the ball is really something. There is a limit to how much an offensive lineman can be glorified. Similar to referees, they are praised for doing a good job when they are not seen or heard. And that is why the aforementioned *Newsweek* commentary was so impressive.

Two years later, Mix's uncanny balance and ferocious blocking paved the way for San Diego's 1963 AFL championship team to lead the league in rushing with 2,201 yards. After playing in numerous AFL All-Star games and championships for the San Diego Chargers, Mix played his last season for John Madden's Oakland Raiders.

"Playing for John was a revelation in that my only other coach, Sid Gilman of the Chargers, was a great coach but was intense and wired tight all of the time and I thought that demeanor was required to be an effective coach. I was wrong. John was less intense, displayed more humor, but was just as effective because you knew he was prepared and had vast knowledge. Being a professional football player was how I most identified myself. It was great to be able to do something that you did well. It was very satisfying to work hard and mold oneself into a superior athlete and then see the results immediately when practice or games began."

By serving as an advocate for retirees' compensation benefits, he is still handling some of the messiest work for his football comrades. And he is only doing so because he had the humility and foresight to think beyond football. Mix may have been a Hall of Fame talent but he was not immune from contemplating and later pursuing a secondary career outside of the hash marks.

Decades after Mix played, another aspiring attorney, Mel Owens, was launching his pro football career in Southern California. A linebacker out of the University of Michigan, Owens was one of the most sought after players in the 1981 NFL Draft. Unbeknown to many modern football fans, Owens was a draftee ahead of Ronnie Lott and a longtime teammate of Eric Dickerson's. Owens warranted so much attention from pro scouts in no small part because of his stellar senior year at the Big House in Ann Arbor, Michigan. It was a season in which he racked up 100 tackles and garnered an honorable All-American mention. Even before playing pro sports, Owens played on one of college football's biggest stages, the Rose Bowl, three times.

"Whatever you do, that is going to be your history. Anytime I wear a Michigan hat, people stop me. Football can't be separated from me. It's a part of me," explains Owens, who now runs a very successful legal practice in Southern California.

After a nine-year career with the Los Angeles Rams in which he amassed 453 tackles, 26.5 sacks, and four interceptions, Owens went back to school to get his law degree at San Francisco-Hastings College of Law. In 2006, Owens partnered with Thomas J. Byrne and Patrick N. Namanny to establish NBO Law, a firm that specializes in helping both current and past professional athletes file claims in the California state court. In addition to being a prominent attorney, Owens often serves as the keynote speaker at many symposiums on the timely issue of former pro athletes seeking workmanship compensation benefits that they rightfully deserve.

"All this attention has percolated recently because of different tools. When you reconnect, you hear more stories. Things come up--good and bad. It traces back to the internet and smartphones; they are ubiquitous. Now it is one world, flattened. Everyone has access to mechanisms."

As both an inside and outside linebacker, Owens experienced first-hand the hazards of trying to make a living in the NFL. Some hits create bumps and bruises that disappear the next morning but others leave their mark months, years, and decades later. In 1988, Owens was relegated to playing in seven games due to a severe ankle injury. Still, he was one of the lucky ones. No physical ailment from his playing days forced him to become bedridden for the rest of his life. And no jarring hit produced devastating neurological side effects to soften his razor sharp intellect.

When Mel left football, he knew he had a healthy brain but one that hadn't been immersed in academia for some time. Transitioning from the NFL to law school was an adjustment. Analyzing case studies and writing law memos required different cognitive skills than plotting a 3-4 defense or executing a weak side blitz. But the two endeavors parallel one another in the sense that they both call for a tireless work ethic.

"Anybody who plays pro sports, the person is driven," says Owens. "You have all the elements that lend itself to another career. You make different decisions based on your opportunities. First and foremost, I had an attorney as an agent. My agent and I have remained close. I speak to him all the time. For me, a post-grad degree was important. It was a question of which one to pursue. School took a lot of effort as I had to ramp up the studying. Lots of things had happened since I left school."

Owens has settled quite nicely into a career in sports law. He is involved in sports, just not in ways that most people are accustomed to seeing athletes staying involved. In a sense, he is coaching athletes on far more important matters in life than sports. He is helping them understand what rights and benefits they are entitled to as former members of professional sports franchises. For Owens, simply conversing about sports related issues with other athletes is an optimal path for his legal career.

"When you have two opportunities [sports and law] and they collide, usually opportunities happen. You gravitate towards what you know. I have played sports all my life. I like being around former players and I see myself. I feel comfortable speaking their language."

Keeping the Spirit of Thurgood Marshall Alive

Alan Page, a paradigm of integrity, diligence, sportsmanship, and excellence, has assumed the Mount Olympus perch of America's legal frontier by sitting on the Supreme Court of Minnesota. Page has a unique perspective that many athletes, attorneys, and scholars don't possess. By not dedicating a lifetime of professionalism to a single discipline or vocation, Page has an inimitably holistic perspective of the world. He also serves as a reminder of how far the country has come in terms of extending equal rights and opportunities to all citizens regardless of skin color.

The year 1954 carries a special meaning for scholars of American legal history. The long overdue racial desegregation of the public school system ensued thanks to the Warren Court's ruling in *Brown v. Board of Education*. The American legal system became more credible when it finally realized that segregated schooling facilities for black and white children were separate and inherently unequal. Thurgood Marshall was the NAACP lawyer who fought the Brown case and later became the first African-American Supreme Court justice. Shortly before Marshall died in January 1993, Page became the first African-American to serve on the Minnesota Supreme Court. That African-American justices such as Page and Marshall have practiced the law at such a high level is a testament to how far the country has come since even the early 1900's when African-Americans were barred from sitting on juries in Southern courthouses. With his unswerving dedication to justice and relentless passion for academia, Page has emerged as a role model in both the African-American and legal communities.

Alas, Page is another former NFL player who simultaneously pursued rigorous intellectual and physical challenges by attending evening law school classes after a full day of football exercises. Before being referred to as Justice Page, he was one of the most gifted defensive players in the annals of NFL history. Any Top Ten List of the NFL's greatest defensive linemen includes Page. While anchoring the Minnesota Vikings defensive line nicknamed the Purple People Eaters, Page was named to nine straight Pro Bowls and received MVP honors in 1971. Page explains his ferocious approach to corralling the ball carriers by stating, "A defensive player should think of himself more as an aggressor, not as a defender." When Page left football, he committed himself to defending justice first as a private attorney and later as a Minnesota Supreme Court Justice.

"I was interested in the law long before my football career began. People would ask me what I wanted to do when I grew up when I was a third or fourth grader. I would say I wanted to be a lawyer, not that I knew what lawyers did or how you became one. But that was sort of in the back of my mind," said Page who grew up in Canton, Ohio--the location of his induction ceremony to the Pro Football Hall of Fame in 1988.

"Over time I developed a sense of the law that it was about solving problems and helping people. As I got older and went off to college and was involved in the Players Association, the law was just a natural fit for me."

While Alan did represent the NFL Players Association on labor issues such as pension and grievance matters, he was not particularly interested in pursuing sports law. As one of the Minnesota Vikings' most prestigious former players, he is still very active in the club's charitable programs and alumnae activities. But he is quite content serving the state of Minnesota with a gavel.

"In my case I don't know that I thought about any parallels [between sports and law]. I think the law is one of those individual interests and I don't think that the sports side of it has much to do with whether or not you have that interest. I think it is life experience that creates the interest independent of sports. Now maybe there are some few who will be motivated to become involved in the law because they want to specifically get into sports related legal areas. I think that's not the kind of thing that is going to really capture one's legal interest. The law is a world onto itself. You either love the law or you don't."

Page pursued his legal studies in a similar fashion to how Ron Mix went about earning his J.D: tackling players by day, textbook readings by night. As Page pursued both endeavors at the same time, he wasn't afforded the luxury of going out to dinner with teammates or relaxing before evening exams. Yet he didn't think of himself as being any different from his fellow classmates who worked in other jobs during the day and went to class at night. If anything, it was just an inconvenience from a logistical standpoint.

"The challenge was finding courses that I needed or wanted to take at times that I was available to take them. Otherwise it was like everybody else who has a full-time job and goes to law school either at night or somehow manages to do it. I don't think there was anything unique there. Certainly law school, even if you are simply a full time student, has its challenges. It can be very demanding but in my case, I happened to love the legal education process. While it was not easy by any stretch of the imagination, when it's something you want to do, it at least makes it fun and interesting.

"The law has been probably the most exciting thing I have ever done. It doesn't have the same physical demands, but in terms of the intellectual challenges, they are quite satisfying."

Taking Law into His Own Hands

David Shand, a native of Cold Lake, Alberta, was selected in the first round of the 1976 NHL Draft by the Atlanta Flames. He ended up playing in 421 NHL games for the Atlanta Flames (now the Calgary

Flames), Toronto Maple Leafs, and Washington Capitals. Today, Shand is heralded as one of the most prominent private attorneys in the entire state of Michigan. A legal scholar with a law degree from the University of Michigan, Shand has also taught sports law courses at his alma mater.

"I'm a litigation and defense attorney. I had to find areas of law that get my heart pumping. I was never going to be a tax attorney," explains Shand. "I love being in court, fighting for guys. I love competing. Stakes are bigger in law [than in hockey]. I have clients of mine sitting in prison. I gave them the best defense that I could. Most guys I played with who are in law wanted to stay competitive."

In a different context, his motivation for entering the legal field was also driven by his fiery competitive spirit. David wanted to prove that hockey players who risked life and limb on a nightly basis could stand up to owners who were profiting from their physical exploits.

"I was a union rep for the minor leagues and NHL. I kept being told that I didn't understand what was going on because I wasn't a lawyer. So when I retired I decided that I would become a lawyer. For me, it was more of a revenge thing than anything else. The league kept telling us we didn't understand anything because we weren't attorneys. Turns out I knew exactly what was going on."

When Shand played in the NHL, the Players Association was led by the surreptitious and corrupt Al Eagleson who believed he could take advantage of "naïve" hockey players. Through serving as the NHLPA's Executive Director for decades, Eagleson duped the players into believing he had their best interests in mind at the bargaining table. Eagleson emerged as a true villain in the history of North American sports. He is right up there with Pete Rose, Marge Schott, and even the fictitious Meyer Wolfsheim. Among other heinous actions, Eagleson pilfered loads of money from player pension funds and disability payments while bilking the Canada Cup of hundreds of thousands of dollars. He also used NHLPA funds to support his lavish lifestyle. *Sports Illustrated* scribe S.L. Price once described Eagleson as a "cocky and high-flying master of the hockey universe."

Eagleson preyed on modestly paid hockey players whose careers were one bone jarring hit away from ending. Shand's career was punctured by such a gut wrenching jolt. After suffering a cracked sinus bone and facial laceration from a Scott Stevens' slap shot during training camp in 1984, Shand knew that he wouldn't be playing hockey forever. A few years later he retired from the game he had been playing since the mid-20th century on frozen ponds in Cold Lake.

After leaving the NHL, Shand went back to the University of Michigan to finish his undergraduate studies. Shortly after receiving his undergrad diploma, he started his courses at Michigan Law School and embarked on his legal career.

"I had to be organized. It's amazing when you focus on what you want to do. Now that I look back, it wasn't that hard. When I first started practicing law, I represented players whom nobody was interested in representing, mainly minor leaguers," said Shand, who once represented Dallas Stars Defenseman Keith Aldridge and New York Islanders Right Wing Steve Webb. "I didn't want to keep advising athletes on issues such as workman compensation. Hockey players are notorious for not taking direction. You can't tell us anything."

Unlike Mix and Owens, Shand left the arena of sports law and opted to devote his legal practice to non-sports related matters such as civil litigation, criminal defense work, divorce and family law as well as trusts and estate settlement. He worked for several private practices before starting his own, Shand Law, in Saline, Michigan.

Despite no longer being immersed in the sports law community, Shand remains very cognizant of the legal issues and financial injustices that run deep through professional sports, particularly hockey. He knows that the NHL Players Association needs sound legal backing so it won't get bullied into submission by the owners. Eagleson is no longer part of the current NHL landscape but opportunistic ownership groups still exercise their predatory inclinations.

"Hockey is plagued by work stoppages. There were two in the nineties and one in each of the first two decades of the 21st century. In 2004 the NHL was ready to burn down the league in order to teach the players a lesson. In all the years of four major sports, I know of not one owner who has lost money. It's just a question of how much money they are going to make. All we ask for is profit sharing or equity participation in the team."

* * *

There are other lawyers in the current American workforce who once devoted tens of thousands of hours mastering an athletic craft. But overall, law is one of the rarest professions for a former professional athlete to enter. Hopefully in the coming years there will be more former athletes who try their hand at law. With the meteoric rise in salaries for pro athletes, it will be interesting to see how many decide to go back to school and start a new career. Even more so than politics, law is a profession that offers scarce opportunity for leveraging former athletic prominence. Yet the legal field offers former athletes an opportunity to either stay connected to the sporting community or pursue other endeavors that offer a refreshingly new perspective on life.

CHAPTER 8
Trading Helmets for Headsets

On April 20, 2012, the Boston Red Sox invited every player who ever donned a Red Sox uniform to come back to help celebrate the hallowed ballpark's 100-Year Anniversary. The list of attendees who were paraded out in front of the Fenway Faithful included such hardball luminaries as Nomar Garciaparra, Dennis Eckersley, Jim Rice, Pedro Martinez, Dwight Evans, Carl Yastrzemski, Mo Vaughn, and Fred Lynn. Afterwards, the general consensus was that the recipient of one of the most raucous standing ovations was none other than Framingham, Massachusetts native Lou Merloni.

Merloni's first and last appearances at Fenway Park were his most memorable. As a kid from Framingham and Providence College, Merloni fulfilled every New England child's dream by belting a home run in his first at bat at Fenway on May 15, 1998 against the Kansas City Royals. As a uniformed retiree during the 2012 ceremony, he was treated like royalty.

The reality is that in between the two milestones, it was a solid career for the utility infielder, who could get the bunt down and not make fans nervous when a ball was hit his way. His career stat line read: 14 home runs, 125 RBI, .271 career batting average. His local popularity is boosted by the fact that he was born within 20 miles of Fenway Park but his emergence as a considerably talented radio and television analyst has made him a celebrity across New England. Whereas dozens of former Red Sox players with more storied careers have faded into obscurity, Merloni looms as a bona fide icon of Red Sox Nation. He hosts a morning show on the Greater Boston sports radio station WEEI and still "pinch hits" by occasionally filling in as an in-game broadcaster. He is one of the most recognizable faces among living Red Sox alums. And he also had the guts to call out Ben Affleck during the 2002 season when the movie star made critical remarks about the team during a televised game broadcast.

The truth is that across many regions of the country, Merloni's story is far from unusual. Announcers and commentators on teams' flagship radio and television stations are veterans of such franchises, but in many cases, not the ones with the glitziest careers. Jerry Remy was a very good middle infielder for the Red Sox (and California Angels). In Greater Boston, he has quite literally become an institution through serving as a color commentator for NESN and ultimately branding his name for business ventures. He is more of a rock star than just about any player whom he analyzes on television--all because of broadcasting and its endless avenues for being exposed to the masses.

On the national level, former utility players have parlayed broadcasting gigs towards becoming multi-millionaire celebrities who are immediately recognized at airports and shopping centers. Many superstars of yesteryear have been able to provide commentary before, during, and after some of the sports world's most prestigious events. Next to coaching, broadcasting is understandably the most natural and logical step for former athletes to take in retirement.

Becoming a Television Icon 20 Miles Southwest of Hartford, Connecticut

The ESPN headquarters in sleepy Bristol, Connecticut is a sports fan's paradise. Nowhere on earth is there a more exhaustive collection of former athletic legends in one place at any given time. Through the years, ESPN has been a pit stop, launching pad, or permanent career move for hundreds, if not thousands, of former athletic stars, starters, and backups interested in pursuing broadcasting careers. Initially, many naysayers were skeptical about whether a station solely dedicated to sports could survive. In no small part due to the expertise offered by former athletes turned broadcasters, the station has emerged as the global leader in sports broadcasting and a multi-billion dollar machine.

"They [former athletes] love the game as much as we do, obviously from a totally different side of the track. But they're big fans too," acknowledged Chris Berman, who was the first renowned ESPN broadcaster and still remains the face of the network to this day. "It's nice to see that after we enjoyed them on the field for so many years that they're in broadcasting. They either want to impart some of what they learned upon viewers or stay involved in the game they loved."

Since ESPN first went on the air in 1979 the list of former athletic greats pulling up to 545 Middle Street in Bristol has included: Michael Irvin, Cris Carter, Ray Lewis, Jerry Rice, Steve Young, Nomar Garciaparra, Barry Larkin, Tony Gwynn, Darren Woodson, Curt Schilling, Marcellus Wiley, Jalen Rose, Rebecca Lobo, Tedy Bruschi, Tino Martinez, Tim Hardaway, Alexi Lalas, Hugh Douglas, Mike Ditka, Keyshawn Johnson, Eric Allen, Ron Jaworski, John Kruk, Mark Mulder, Magic Johnson, Chris Mullin, Nancy Lieberman, Paul Silas, David Justice, Kurt Rambis, Rick Sutcliffe, Eric Dickerson, Orel Hershiser, Antonio Pierce, Joe Morgan, Matt Light, Brandi Chastain, Jamal Mashburn, Patrick McEnroe, Bill Walton, Dave Winfield, and too many others to name.

Those are the many stars who have chosen to spend at least a portion of their post-playing careers broadcasting for the station known as the Worldwide Leader in Sports. However, similar to many regional broadcasters, some of the former athletes with less gaudy resumes are the ones who have shined brightest in front of the camera. When younger generations of sports fans turn on Sports Center, they are so inundated with images of Trent Dilfer, Tim Legler, Tom Jackson, and Barry Melrose that they understandably may be under the impression that such athletes were superstars in their day. The truth is that for many of ESPN's celebrity broadcasters, their keen insight likely stems from spending thousands of hours observing teammates rather than playing alongside them.

Some football fans may look at Jackson and Dilfer and think they are the luckiest guys in the sporting world for having seamlessly transitioned from playing to broadcasting. Both players had fairly lengthy careers and were the rare pro football players whose best professional days turned out to be ahead of them when they retired. It now seems that lucrative and successful broadcasting careers will sustain them all the way until their final retirement from professional life. However, at times they have been some of the unluckiest individuals in the world for heartbreaking reasons.

Jackson had a very productive 14-year career as a linebacker for the Denver Broncos. He made three consecutive Pro Bowl appearances from 1977-1979 and compiled 20 career interceptions. But in early August 1997, football was the last thing on Jackson's mind. His nine-year-old daughter, Andrea Jackson, died in a head-on car collision along Interstate 25 in California. Dilfer also experienced life-altering tragedy when his five-year-old son died of a rare heart disease in spring 2003. From watching their charismatic facial expressions and infectious smiles on Sundays in the fall, fans would never know that their lives have been plagued with so much tumult and misery.

Jackson and Dilfer stayed true to their football roots by taking the hardest hits life can offer and then getting back on their feet as nationally recognized sports broadcasters. They could have slipped outside of the public consciousness and led private lives with their families. But both longtime NFL veterans knew they could entertain so many Americans with their natural broadcasting skills while establishing themselves as iconic television personalities. And the ESPN studio was a vehicle for staying involved in a game that was their passion and livelihood for so many years.

Jackson has paired with Berman on immensely entertaining ESPN football shows including Prime Time and the Blitz. Pigskin lovers equate fall Sunday evenings with TJ and Boomer's rants, jokes, gasps, and trademark sayings. In addition to his Sunday night performances with Berman, TJ also participates in the Monday Night Football pregame show, Monday Night Countdown.

In his time at ESPN, Berman has seen hundreds of athletes come and go. Jackson has been at his side through the Joe Montana years, Dallas Cowboys dynasty and, more recently, the New England Patriots era of dominance. In the storied history of the revolutionary television station, no broadcast partners have worked together as long as Berman and Jackson.

"Tom Jackson and I have been together 27 years. Carson and McMahon were 31. We've long since passed Desi and Lucy. Tommy and I complete each other's sentences. We listen to the same sort of music even though we grew up differently. He's become one of my best friends," commented Berman, who can be considered the godfather of ESPN.

They certainly did come from very different backgrounds. Jackson grew up in a working class district of Cleveland while Berman was raised in a Jewish upper-middle class household in Greenwich, Connecticut. As a child, Berman went to overnight camp in Maine while Jackson was a phenomenal high school athlete who went on to play football at the University of Louisville for head coach Lee Corso.

"We've seen each other get married and have kids. We love football together. We'll watch a game and we'll talk about a lot of his experiences with 14 years with the Broncos and I remember a lot of the games so it's kind of interesting," added Berman.

Just like he was as an undersized linebacker going up against bigger and stronger opponents, Jackson is fearless in the broadcast booth. He didn't have a Hall of Fame career but still felt comfortable making the audacious claim that the New England Patriots "hate their coach" at the start of the 2003 season when coach Bill Belichick had released popular veteran safety Lawyer Milloy. Jackson has also not shied away from publicly criticizing Chicago Bears All-Pro quarterback Jay Cutler. Several decades removed from his last NFL snap, Jackson knows that the country identifies him as a broadcaster first, player second. He feels empowered to call out even those who may have accomplished more in their playing days.

Both Jackson and Dilfer have come into their own as broadcasters at the right time. The NFL has carved out its niche on America's most important network stations. NFL television broadcasts blare across thousands of sports bars and millions of living rooms on Sunday afternoons. Most sports fans agree there is no better sport to watch on television than football. Some even say it is better on television than in person. The hits are louder and the plays are more visible. When Jackson was a broadcasting novice in the late 1980's, even he was taken aback by the power of the medium. And this was before NFL Redzone and sprawling flat screen televisions.

"The first time I ever worked with Tom, it was the first Sunday. We were watching nine games and 15 minutes in there's a big hit. He goes 'oh man look at that!' I said, 'Tommy, that's what you did for 14 years.' He goes, 'yeah I guess so but look at that, that's an amazing hit.' So we had a good time then," recalled Berman.

Good times were what Trent Dilfer needed when he was in the waning days of his NFL career in 2003. After his son passed away, the depressed quarterback was putting on excessive weight and regularly drinking himself to sleep. He still managed to get back up on his feet and compete against world class athletes for a few more years before retiring from the NFL at the close of the 2007 season. Having experienced so much personal torment, Dilfer could easily have suffered unbearable emotional and physical pain in the excessive free time he had upon retiring. Instead, he tapped into a newfound set of broadcasting talents.

As a player, Dilfer had moments of promise and stardom sprinkled amongst mediocrity. He was the sixth overall pick of the 1994 NFL Draft and quarterbacked the Baltimore Ravens to a Super Bowl victory during the 2000 season. When his playing career was all said and done, his longevity did ultimately yield 20,518 passing yards. But his greater calling in life would be analyzing the game he had played for over a quarter century.

After a journeyman career for a spate of franchises including the Tampa Bay Buccaneers, Baltimore Ravens, Seattle Seahawks, Cleveland Browns, and San Francisco 49ers, Dilfer has emerged as a legitimate television star. Interestingly, some of Dilfer's colleagues at ESPN who had more illustrious athletic careers, such as former quarterback Steve Young, don't have nearly as much of a visible presence on the daily programming schedule. The station's annual week-long Super Bowl coverage involves copious amounts of Dilfer's insightful analysis. Similar to Jackson, Dilfer is not hesitant to use the sporting world's most visible stage to criticize even the brightest of NFL stars.

Whereas Dilfer is *one* of ESPN's chief football analysts, Barry Melrose *is* ESPN's hockey analyst. On Sports Center, a hockey conversation is synonymous with Melrose's trademark mullet and thick Canadian accent. He is the authoritative voice on all things hockey and an iconic sportscaster for the world's most prestigious sports broadcasting network. Few NHL alums have as visible a presence as Melrose. Legends such as Gordie Howe, Brett Hull, and Mark Messier can walk around more anonymously. Had Melrose never broadcasted (and coached) he would not be competing with Barry Manilow for the most pop-ups on a "Barry M" search on Google. Melrose potted ten goals in his NHL career. Many NHL first liners net their first 10 goals of a season by Thanksgiving.

Blessed with good looks and even better vocal cords, Tim Legler has remained a fixture of ESPN's basketball crew. He was a threat from three-point range but bounced around a number of teams before suffering a career devastating back injury. Legler, commonly known as Legs, played with Anthony Mason, Mitch Richmond, Rod Strickland, Calbert Cheaney, Jeff Hornacek, and Jim Jackson. Unlike those former stars who walk around public areas in relative anonymity, Legler is now the one who gets the star treatment in public.

The Mount Olympus of sports broadcasters includes the likes of play-by-play announcers such as Bob Costas, Howard Cosell, Al Michaels, and Berman. While no former athletes have assumed the role of play-by-play announcer, many have joined the ranks of the most iconic sports broadcasters in the history of television through providing color commentary. And the exploding popularity of ESPN has helped some former journeymen athletes rise to such a prominent level in the media industry.

Broadcasters Who Once Hated the Media

It is no secret that the relationship between players and the media can often be a contentious one. There have been ugly incidents such as Los Angeles Rams quarterback Jim Everett physically assaulting TV host Jim Rome during a live on-air episode of Rome's show in 1994. A few years earlier, late *Boston Globe* columnist Will McDonough punched New England Patriots cornerback Raymond Clayborn in the locker room following a game. Another *Boston Globe* columnist, Dan Shaughnessy, once referred to Red Sox infielder Jose Offerman as a "piece of junk." Those tales represent an extreme, but the general nature of their respective professions dictates that the reporter and the athlete stand as adversaries. While the television/radio media often become chummier with athletes in their respective markets, print and web journalists are paid to hold athletes accountable for their transgressions both on and off the field. In the locker rooms, athletes often view obligatory interviews with the media as a thorn in their side. When biting criticism hits the airwaves and printing press, the media goes from an annoyance to a personal torment. So it is somewhat surprising that even those athletes who formerly despised the media in their playing days, such as Jim Rice and Nomar Garciaparra, have joined its ranks.

Red Sox legend Jim Rice was not particularly fond of the press and the feelings were reciprocal. Younger New Englanders think of Rice as an affable middle-aged gentleman who serves his role well as ambassador to Red Sox Nation. He shows up to nearly every Red Sox team-related function and is a nightly regular on the Fenway Park jumbo screen. Even when he is broadcasting pre- and post-game shows, he still refers to the Red Sox as "we."

Older New Englanders don't have such a short-term memory. They remember a former slugger who was at times rather rude and arrogant to the Boston media. They know that when Rice played, he did not have the beloved and polished image that is associated with other 1980's hardball legends such as Tom Seaver and Cal Ripken. Red Sox fans who were around in the 1980's remember when Rice ripped the shirt off *Hartford Courant* reporter Steve Fainaru during an altercation in the visiting clubhouse of the Oakland Coliseum. Pressured to file his story by deadline, Fainaru reported back to the press box with his shirt in tatters.

Rice, an African-American man from South Carolina, came to Boston in 1974 just as the Boston Busing Crisis was starting. Racial strife enveloped Beantown. It was not an easy time for a black baseball player to embark on his rookie campaign in a city that was notoriously racist. Understandably, Rice may have felt uncomfortable relating to the media during such a controversial time. Over the years, Rice would show signs of cooperating with the Boston press and carrying himself in a more cordial manner. But not even Rice's biggest fans could deny the fact that he had a frosty relationship with Boston's media members.

Yet years after his career was cut short because of a devastating wrist injury, Rice has become a fixture on the NESN telecasts for over a decade. Perceived as grumpy and crass as a player, Rice couldn't be any different in his television work for the shows on NESN, the flagship station for the Boston Red Sox. He is entertaining, insightful, and charming. His smile has been described as infectious. He will identify himself as a member of the Red Sox but not shy away from criticizing current players when such objective assessments are due.

"I may have only worked alongside Jim once at NESN but I will say as a viewer this was not a natural career move for him and he has made significant improvement," says *Boston Globe* columnist Bob Ryan.

However, even years removed from his playing days, Rice hasn't forgotten his less than favorable reputation in Boston. During his Hall of Fame induction speech in 2009, Rice, a former high school student union president, acknowledged the irony of a former media hater such as himself becoming part of the institution.

"By now you may be wondering how did I get such a notorious reputation with the media. Well you see, the media often asked me questions about my [fellow] players. I refused to be the media's mouthpiece. Of course my stance didn't really make any media friends. I came to Boston to play professional baseball and that's what I did, and I did it well until I retired in 1989. And who would have ever guessed that I would be working in media at NESN sitting across the desk from Tom Caron, allowing all of you to see my winning smile?"

By the late 1990's Rice's protégé, Nomar Garciaparra, was arguably the most popular Red Sox player since Ted Williams. Amongst New Englanders from Presque Isle, Maine to Cumberland, Rhode Island, Garciaparra was the beloved face of the franchise. He reeled off a 30-game hitting streak during his rookie year and posted a .372 batting average in 2000. Little Leaguers tried to emulate his off-balance throws from deep in the hole at shortstop. Unlike the majority of big leaguers, he ran out every single ground ball and infield pop-up.

And off the field he endeared himself to Red Sox Nation with his humility and understated charitable work. Even when it became apparent that Garciaparra's days in a Boston Red Sox uniform were numbered, he didn't forget about some of the region's most needy residents. In May 2004, the *Boston Globe* published a story profiling homeless men who enjoyed watching the Red Sox every night at the local Pine Street Inn. The Red Sox games gave them some relief from their often depressing and burdensome daily lives. Unfortunately, the shelter could only afford a small 17-inch TV for residents to huddle around while they watched in the second-floor common room. Without a single press release, Nomar took it upon himself to send over a brand new plasma flat screen for the gentlemen to enjoy.

He was even a darling of the local media before his relationship with the infamous Knights of the Keyboard turned sour during the latter portion of his Red Sox career. Over time, the face of the franchise grew tired of reporters swarming around his locker every day and pestering him with questions about his frequent injuries, occasional batting slumps, and looming contract issues. When Garciaparra was jettisoned to the Chicago Cubs on July 31, 2004 in a historic multi-team trade, most of the Boston sports media celebrated his departure. By that time, the feelings were mutual. Garciaparra had publicly expressed his frustration with having to endure the media crazed Boston baseball experience. He would frequently complain that there were too many credentialed media members in the Red Sox clubhouse. During post-game interviews, reporters became accustomed to his one word answers, stares, and scowls. After Boston beat the Oakland A's in Game 4 of the 2003 Division Series, the shortstop got on the bus headed towards Logan Airport. The Red Sox were bound for Oakland and a win away from advancing to the ALCS. In front of his pumped up teammates, Garciaparra asked, "Why is everyone so happy? As soon as we lose, everyone's just going to rip us." At one point, he had the Red Sox clubhouse staff set up a taped red line in front of his locker. When Nomar was behind that line, even the most intrepid journalists did not dare to get a sound bite from him. Many felt that Garciaparra, who struggled with Obsessive Compulsive Disorder, would be happier and more relaxed playing for a team in his native region of Southern California, an area where baseball players don't go to work every day under relentless media scrutiny. No one accused him of being a nasty person. He was just more of the reclusive type who couldn't accept the fact that 24/7 public scrutiny came with being the face of the Boston Red Sox franchise.

Naturally, many folks considered it ironic that upon retirement, Garciaparra was pining for a broadcasting gig after he experienced an often acrimonious relationship with the Boston media. Literally hours after he retired in March 2010, Garciaparra was hired by ESPN as one of its newly minted commentators. The following day, the *Boston Globe* published Shaughnessy's column that read: "In yesterday's sorry spirit of disingenuousness and hypocrisy, Garciaparra announced that he has taken a job with ESPN. This makes him a member of the media, which is like Sarah Palin telling us she is going to be chairman of the Democratic National Committee. In good times and bad, Garciaparra was unnecessarily difficult in all interactions with the media. It made no sense, given the fawning coverage he received (and deserved) for the first seven years of his career."

As a broadcaster for ESPN, Garciaparra nudges players for post-game remarks and makes critical on-air assessments of former colleagues. He loathed being on the other end of such dialogue. Even after belting a grand slam or making a game-saving catch, Garciaparra felt disinclined to provide any sort of colorful commentary in the clubhouse afterwards. He loved muttering clichés and delivering seemingly scripted remarks on his performance. Shaughnessy once commented how: "He [Garciaparra] is never going to give us the Ali or Barkley sound bite. He spoonfeeds vanilla, even when the moment calls for Cherry Garcia or Chocolate Chip Cookie Dough. We're never going to know how he really feels."

So what is even more ironic is that Garciaparra has flourished in his new role as baseball analyst for ESPN. He not only has emerged as a regular on the channel's trademark show Baseball Tonight, but he has also carved out his personal niche by broadcasting from the College World Series and Little League World Series. He even got to interview Derek Jeter days before the Yankee captain reached the 3,000 hit milestone. But before having the chance to serve as one of ESPN's chief baseball experts, Garciaparra had to prove himself as a broadcaster. It didn't matter that he was at one time considered quite possibly the best right-handed hitter in the American League since Joe DiMaggio.

In early March 2010, Garciaparra auditioned in Bristol, Connecticut for an ESPN baseball analyst position. Just like when he played, Garciaparra stayed humble and grounded. He told his evaluators: "Please let me know how I am. We're in Connecticut, near New York City, and I'm used to hearing how bad I am from trash-talking Yankees fans. You're not going to hurt my feelings."

At ESPN, Garciaparra couldn't be more different from how he was as a player. He still prepares diligently hours before performance time through conducting tireless backroom research. But on the air, Garciaparra is visibly more relaxed and animated as he offers sincere insight on hitting, base running, and potential trades. As he has grown more comfortable in his broadcasting position, he has become more direct and assertive in providing objective analysis of former teammates and opponents. He is talking baseball, the game that has consumed the better portion of his life for nearly four decades. After his broadcasting career got underway, Garciaparra confided to the Boston Globe's Shira Springer that: "Anybody who knew me while I was playing knew I could talk about baseball for hours. Now I'm able to explain the game as an analyst. I love the game, and I love talking about it. I wish I had done part of this while I was playing."

Life has been very sweet for Garciaparra during retirement. He is married to former soccer star Mia Hamm and has raised twin daughters. When he comes back to Fenway Park and Boston for events, a throng of uproarious fans awaits him. He is now ESPN analyst Nomar Garciaparra and the dark days of July 2004 seem like a lifetime ago.

In the end, both Rice and Garciaparra could have leveraged their well-deserved fame and wealth towards many other professional endeavors. But their love of the game was so strong that they embarked on a line of work that formerly repulsed them. And today they are waiting in line alongside their former adversaries for food in the same workplace cafeterias.

Calling Out Former Bosses and Comrades

When one works for a national broadcast team, there is no room for transparent favoritism. It doesn't matter whether or not such a former athlete gave blood, sweat, and tears for a coach and teammates. He or she is now being paid to criticize former colleagues in one of the most highly visible arenas in sports.

Every year, the New England Patriots expect to play the Indianapolis Colts at the halfway point of the season. The 2009 season was no different. That Patriots team approached their midseason showdown against the Colts feeling very grateful to have their franchise quarterback Tom Brady back at the helm after he missed the prior season due to injury. New England was off to a hot start, going 6-2 with only razor close road losses to the New York Jets and Denver Broncos.

The NBC Sunday Night Football Game between the Patriots and Colts lived up to the hype. The Patriots found themselves ahead 34-21 with 4:12 left in regulation. After Indianapolis made it 34-28 and New England faced a 4th and 2 from its own 28-yard line, Belichick inexplicably opted for his team to go for the first down rather than punt it away. The Patriots couldn't convert the first down and the Colts went on to score the game winning touchdown. For the Patriots, it was a devastating loss that would prove to be a turning point in their season.

Belichick's longtime loyal followers Tedy Bruschi, Rodney Harrison, and Christian Fauria, were serving as broadcasters at the time. All three broadcasters, and in particular Bruschi, took to the airwaves to criticize their former coach. Bruschi's rather pointed remarks went as follows:

"As a former defender on that team, I would've cared less about the result of that fourth-down attempt. The decision to go for it would be enough to make my blood boil for weeks. Bill Belichick sent a message to his defense. He felt that his chances were better to go for it on his own 28-yard line than to punt it away and make Peyton Manning have to drive the majority of the field to win the game.

"I would look at this decision as a lack of confidence in our ability as a defensive unit to come up with a big play to win the game. If I'm Jerod Mayo, Gary Guyton, Darius Butler, Jonathan Wilhite, Brandon Meriweather and Brandon McGowan -- to name a few -- I'm wondering why we weren't given the chance to do what we've been coached to do ever since the first day we practiced.

"Sure, Tom Brady and the offense loved the vote of confidence that their head coach was giving them, but the message sent to the defense was loud and clear. It was a message of doubt. A message that will be with the entire defensive unit--coaches and players--until a situation comes up like this again. And I'm not talking about stopping the New York Jets with Mark Sanchez. I'm talking about the biggest of games on the biggest of stages.

"Belichick will take full responsibility for his decision. That will help little. He is going to have to rebuild the feeling of confidence in his defensive unit. Right now, every member of the defense is wishing they had the chance to stop Manning and the Colts offense on Sunday night. That's how I see it and that's how championship defenses should see it."

Bruschi made these explosive comments for ESPN on November 16, 2009. He was an employee of ESPN, working for NFL Live as a studio analyst. A year earlier, he was a linebacker for the nearly undefeated New England Patriots, sweating profusely during sweltering summer training camps and risking serious bodily harm to please Belichick. As a player, Bruschi was one of Belichick's most trustworthy and loyal veterans who never criticized his coach publicly; now he was one of his fiercest critics. In 2009, Bruschi's allegiance was to ESPN. Broadcasting, not playing football, was currently paying his bills. He was getting paid for articulating his sincere comments, especially during moments of great controversy. Sincere opinions meant higher ratings and happy bosses. He was a broadcaster now, not a Patriot.

A couple of years later, during the end of the infamous 2011 Red Sox train wreck season, Curt Schilling was serving as a baseball analyst for ESPN. In 2004 and 2007, Schilling played an instrumental role in helping the Red Sox win the World Series. However in front of the camera, Schilling felt inclined to foretell the nightmarish fortunes of his former colleagues. He made the blunt (and accurate) prediction that the Red Sox would not make the postseason. There was no public reaction from players but Red Sox skipper Terry Francona responded that he didn't give a [expletive]. In this case, Schilling's intrepid move to remain an objective member of the media served as a paradigm of professionalism.

* * *

When they're playing, they participate in a seemingly endless string of interviews. Some athletes (Ray Lewis, Shaquille O'Neal) can't wait before they retire to be on the other end of such conversations. Going from playing to broadcasting is such a natural transition that many current players jump at the chance to serve in a cameo role behind the microphone when their teams are not playing in postseason competition. It may sting not playing in the World Series, but the next best thing is to be providing commentary on the event for tens of millions of viewers worldwide.

"It [broadcasting] was definitely fun. It was an eye-opening experience to see how hard it is and see how much work is required to put a baseball game on TV. It would definitely be something I would be interested in doing again," said veteran catcher A.J. Pierzynski, who filled in nicely for FOX's broadcasting team during the 2011 postseason.

"What I enjoyed most was getting to see how it worked, how games are put on TV. I learned a lot about things you need to know as far as production and the science of it. Plus I got to watch baseball and talk about baseball."

Of course the national broadcasting jobs are few and far between. Not every retired athlete can be Charles Barkley on TNT or Dan Marino on CBS. The overwhelming majority of former pro athletes who go behind the mike do so for the networks that cover their former teams. Many teams even have ownership rights of the stations that broadcast their games. So therefore most spectators don't blink an eye when Jim Rice still refers to the Red Sox as "us" or "we." He is still serving as an extension of the only team that he ever donned a uniform for. Yet sometimes even long tenured veterans of a team have to wait months or years to get the invite to audition for the station that broadcasts their former team's games

Whether it is done on a temporary basis for August preseason NFL games on the local network channel or full-time at ESPN, broadcasting is a viable way to continue living the dream of being involved in sports. For many, it is the perfect way to fill up their professional days prior to leaving the workforce for good.

CHAPTER 9
A New Position: the Front Office

It seemed to be the ultimate irony: the indisputably greatest basketball player ever was managing quite possibly the worst basketball team ever. The 2011-2012 Charlotte Bobcats were the ultimate train wreck of a team, finishing with an abysmal 7-59 record during the truncated season. The executive largely in charge of assembling the roster and managing personnel decisions was Michael Jordan. His abject failure as Charlotte's chief executive shed light on what many already knew: sometimes the best players aren't necessarily the best managers of people.

Top player personnel positions in the NBA have often been occupied by former superstars. The list includes Joe Dumars, Larry Bird, Danny Ainge, Jerry West, Elgin Baylor, Isaiah Thomas, Chris Mullin, Kevin McHale, and Jordan. No other sport has had so many past legends occupying chief managerial positions yet most of those aforementioned stars have struggled to keep their teams competitive. While it is an extreme example, Jordan's struggles do reflect a larger trend in basketball. Some of the all-time great NBA players have become mediocre if not poor executive managers.

Elgin Baylor--who once scored 71 points in a game and was the league's first overall pick in 1958--was hired by the basketball operations office of the Los Angeles Clippers in 1986. In 22 seasons with Baylor as Vice President of Basketball Operations, the Clippers finished over .500 only twice and won just one playoff series. The sharpshooting Mullin was the face of the Golden State Warriors franchise for years but still experienced an acrimonious tenure as the team's general manager before he parted ways with the organization in 2009.

The most ghastly horror story belongs to Isaiah Thomas who drove the New York Knicks into the ground while personally exhibiting morally reprehensible behavior. "One of the biggest regrets of my life" is how Thomas described his inability to make the Knicks a winner. Despite having one of the league's highest payrolls, the Knicks failed to ever win a playoff game while Thomas was their President of Basketball Operations. Off the court, Thomas faced an explosive $10 million sexual harassment scandal over claims that he acted inappropriately towards fellow employees.

Given the avalanche of failure on behalf of the previously mentioned individuals, those who do succeed in management deserve extra merit. Success on the court does not necessarily translate to success in the corner office. That being said, executives in other sports have shown that success playing and success managing do not have to be mutually exclusive.

Baseball

To many observers, it seems odd that the majority of general managers/ directors of player personnel in the NBA, NFL, and NHL are former pro athletes in their respective sports while their counterparts in MLB are guys who mostly never played past high school. Baseball is the most inclusive of all the sports in terms of allowing non former players a chance to assume roles at upper levels of management. None of the whiz kids who have recently become general managers (Theo Epstein, Mark Shapiro, Josh Byrnes, Jed Hoyer, Jon Daniels) ever played professional baseball. The ultimate irony is that the special assistants to the general manager are often former All-Stars. The seemingly daily growing list includes such names as Pedro Martinez, Jason Varitek, Ken Griffey Jr., Jim Thome, Felipe Alou, and Aaron Sele.

In this sense, Nolan Ryan, the man who recently finished his tenure as the Texas Rangers Vice President of Baseball Operations, is an anomaly. Known as one of the greatest players in franchise history, Ryan has been just as valuable to the team through serving as a chief executive in the front office. After Texas annually posted mediocre results in the early 2000's and fell short of the postseason, Ryan has overseen the team's acquisition of new and exciting talent so that fans no longer miss Juan Gonzalez, Rafael Palmeiro, Will Clark, and Ivan Rodriguez. As an executive, Ryan oversaw the makeover of a roster that catapulted the Rangers to consecutive American League pennants in 2010 and 2011.

In his sixties, the Ryan Express hasn't lost his fastball--literally. Prior to Game 1 of the 2010 American League Championship Series, the 63-year-old threw out the first pitch by humming an 86 mile per hour fastball to catcher Ivan Rodriguez. Traditionally, most people who toss the first pitch actually toss it, floating 30 mile per hour pitches that bear the trajectory of a parabola. Ryan's first pitch was an implicit reminder to his players that the man watching over their first postseason run in a decade still had his fiery zeal for competition. After starting his career during the Lyndon B. Johnson administration and ending it in Bill Clinton's first term, Ryan still has the burning desire to compete on the field himself, even if he is the most powerful executive in the organization.

Hours after the ceremonial first pitch, Ryan acknowledged, "It's horrible. The two toughest things I found in sports are to watch your children perform and be involved with a team of this nature and not have any control over what's going on, that you're strictly a spectator."

Even though he doesn't play anymore, Ryan is still the face of the franchise. During nationally televised postseason games played at the Rangers Ballpark in Arlington, Ryan is caught on camera sandwiched between George W. Bush and George H.W. Bush in front row seats behind the on-deck circle. The younger Bush is an avid baseball fan and used to be a partial owner of the Rangers. Over the years, players from opposing teams have even tried to snag press credentials in order to shake hands with a Hall of Fame pitcher who hurled a record seven no-hitters.

After initially turning to cattle ranching and business ventures in retirement, Ryan found his niche in the front office. Management may not be a substitute for playing, but it allows Ryan to stay intimately connected to baseball and keep his former team relevant in a football-crazed region of America.

Hockey

After playing 22 years for the Detroit Red Wings and helping the franchise end its long Stanley Cup drought, Steve Yzerman figured he would have a good chance to be hired as Detroit's next general manager. As a quiet 18-year-old kid from Cranbrook, British Columbia, Yzerman seamlessly transitioned to playing in one of North America's most ballyhooed sports environments, Detroit, a.k.a. Hockeytown. He potted 692 goals and assisted on 1,063 of his teammates' lucky strikes. In 1997, Yzerman led the Red Wings to their first Stanley Cup victory in 42 years by sweeping the Philadelphia Flyers in the final round. The Yzerman captained Red Wings would go on to sweep the Washington Capitals in the following year's Stanley Cup Finals.

Stevie Y was to Detroit what Mickey Mantle was to New York City: an outrageously beloved superstar who played his first and last game in the same sports-obsessed city. Yzerman was highly regarded as one of the most popular athletes in Detroit sports history, having led the Red Wings to championships in 1997, 1998, and 2002. Through the years, he was just as popular if not more so than other Detroit legends such as Barry Sanders, Al Kaline, and Joe Dumars.

After working in Detroit's front office for a number of years after playing, Yzerman realized that there were other executives above him on the totem pole that were more likely to get the nod first. He was not discouraged. When he was offered the position of becoming the Tampa Bay Lightning's new general manager in 2010, he jumped at the opportunity, acknowledging that "throughout my playing career and into my first four years of retirement I always had a goal to run a hockey team." It became apparent to him that in Detroit, such a dream would not become reality for a long time.

Leaving the Red Wings for the Tampa Bay G.M. job was not an easy decision. Detroit was all he knew for a quarter century and it would be weird to consider the Red Wings one of his competitors. During his introductory press conference in Tampa Bay, Yzerman acknowledged that "it was very difficult to leave the Red Wings. I had been there my entire career, surrounded by good people that really protected me and looked after me. That's my home and where my children were born."

As a general manager, Yzerman would have to make other difficult decisions, some of which tested his new team's loyalty to storied franchise players. Shortly after the 2012-2013 season concluded, Yzerman opted to buy out the remaining seven years of Vincent Lecavalier's contract. Similar to Yzerman, Lecavalier sweated through thousands of grueling shifts for the same organization before eventually moving on to represent an opponent. The Lightning decided that it made more sense to keep another aging franchise cornerstone, Martin St. Louis, while allowing Lecavalier to sign with the Eastern Conference rival Philadelphia Flyers as a free agent.

While the sample size has been small, Yzerman's body of work has been impressive thus far. In 2010, he took over a downtrodden Tampa Bay franchise that was mired in a prolonged slump. During the very next season, the Lightning was a goal away from advancing to the Stanley Cup Finals for the second time in franchise history.

While the Lightning hasn't been around for that long, Yzerman is not the only former NHL superstar to serve as its G.M. During its inaugural season, the Lightning named Hall of Famer Phil Esposito as its first ever general manager after he campaigned tirelessly for the NHL to establish its first franchise in Florida.

Esposito was a trailblazer of the NHL's Southern Strategy that called for the league to tap into new markets across America's Sunbelt. Some skeptics believed that ice would melt in the Southern heat and natives would always choose the beach over the rink. Esposito knew that a 70 degree indoor rink would be 70 degrees regardless of whether it was -20 or 90 degrees outside. If teams proved to be victorious, the fans would put aside their towels and sunscreen. While the Phoenix Coyotes and Nashville Predators have struggled to stay financially solvent, franchises in Raleigh, Anaheim, Dallas, Los Angeles, and Tampa Bay have all won league titles since the NHL moved south. There are now two Floridian NHL franchises with the Florida Panthers being the other.

"I've done a lot of things in the game, but that [jumpstarting the Tampa Bay Lightning] was my greatest achievement," said Esposito, who retired as one of the NHL's all-time leading goal scorers. "I was running the New York Rangers. I had three years left on my contract when they fired me in 1989. I didn't know what to do with myself. I was on the marketing committee of the NHL as a player and as a general manager and I knew they wanted to expand in the South."

Esposito had another memorable pioneering experience as Tampa's G.M. when he signed female goaltender Manon Rheaume to a temporary contract so she could suit up for some of the Lightning's preseason games prior to the 1992 and 1993 seasons. While many viewed it as a crafty publicity stunt, Rheaume was a world class goalie and Esposito gave her a chance to compete against some of the best players in the world.

Before Esposito broke the gender barrier in the NHL (albeit for a couple preseason games), he was breaking barriers as a player. In 1969, he became the first NHL player to surpass 100 points in a season. Two years later, Esposito broke the NHL single season scoring record by netting 76 goals.

A couple years after Esposito retired from the NHL, another Bruins superstar would launch his Hall of Fame career. Similar to Esposito, Cam Neely was a fellow Canadian who used his strong physical frame to dominate play at the offensive end. Despite having his career curtailed due to devastating injuries, Neely still scored 395 career goals en route to becoming one of the greatest Right Wings to ever play the game.

While he has done television and movie cameos and started a wonderful charitable foundation in his name, Neely has been one of the individuals most responsible for getting the Boston Bruins past the second round of the playoffs. After Neely retired from playing, the Bruins had some talented teams. During their best years, they would get upset in the Eastern Conference Semifinals. During their off years, the Bruins were relegated to the back burner of New England sports. When the Patriots and Red Sox were on top of the sports world in the early years of the 21st century, the Bruins were on the brink of irrelevancy. The team typically plays its home games on Thursday and Saturday nights. For the Thursday games, the team at one point had to sell half price tickets. The current flagship radio station of the Boston Bruins, 98.5 The Sports Hub, was not in existence, which meant that the B's got negligible time on mainstream airwaves.

Neely returned to the Bruins organization in September 2007 when he joined the front office as a vice president. Under his leadership, the Bruins drafted and developed young stars Milan Lucic, David Krejci, and Tuukka Rask. The overall consensus around hockey was that there was no better person than Neely to direct player personnel matters for the Bruins.

Yet for a while, the Bruins still couldn't skate past the second round of the Stanley Cup Playoffs. In 2009, they fell to the Carolina Hurricanes in the second round and the next year the Philadelphia

Flyers came back from a 3-0 second round series deficit to prevent the Bruins from advancing to the Eastern Conference Finals.

During Neely's first season as team president, the Black and Gold ended their 39-year championship drought by defeating the Vancouver Canucks in the 2011 Stanley Cup Finals. The Bruins re-emerged as the most popular team in Boston. None of the other Boston teams got as many New Englanders to come out and celebrate their respective titles. Once again the Bruins were the hottest ticket in Boston.

Football

John Elway was 37-years-old and in his 15th season when he won his first Super Bowl. He was one of the greatest quarterbacks of all time, but he lost his first three Super Bowls to the Giants, Redskins, and 49ers by a combined score of 136-40 and was labeled as a guy who couldn't even come close to winning the big game. He was 38 and in his 16th and final season when he won his other championship ring. No legendary career in the history of professional sports has ended on a better note.

For the first decade of retirement, Elway mostly stayed away from football. Even though he pursued business endeavors bearing scant resemblance to football, he still remained the face of a Denver Broncos franchise that went from a perennial contender to mediocrity without his services. By the time he took over as the team's Executive Vice President of Football Operations in 2011, the Broncos were looking for their first playoff victory since January 2006 when they eliminated the New England Patriots in the AFC Divisional Round. The last time the Broncos had gone through such a rough stretch was in the pre-Elway era of the 1970's.

As one of the chief executives of the Broncos, Elway quickly made a splash by revitalizing a once proud organization. He tabbed John Fox to be the head coach and prudently used the second overall pick in the 2011 NFL Draft to select gifted linebacker Von Miller to serve as a linchpin of the defense. Elway's biggest move came in March 2012. He had the foresight to realize that Tim Tebow's weaknesses would get exposed the more he competed against NFL defenses. Tebow, one of the most polarizing athletes of the modern generation, was not going to lead the Broncos to multiple championships like Elway had done in the Mile High City. He was a flash in the pan and Elway knew it. The new head of football operations jettisoned Tebow to the New York Jets and acquired Peyton Manning in one of the league's most historic free agent signings on March 21, 2012. The following off-season, Elway signed another star veteran, receiver Wes Welker, to form a quarterback/wide receiver tandem for the ages.

The Broncos may or may not win a Super Bowl or AFC Title with Elway at the helm. Winning the conference means knocking off powerhouse teams such as New England, Baltimore, and Houston. But the important thing is that the Orange Crush returned to respectability thanks to the man who brought them there in the first place.

***

Player personnel decisions are often the hardest ones to make in sports--especially during contract negotiations. At that stage, it's strictly a numbers business. Ironically, current athletes are encouraged to let their agents handle the number crunching and bargaining work. Maybe that is partially why many former athletes who become executives find it challenging to engage in such business matters.

CHAPTER 10
Those Who Won't Retire

For aging athletes, the goal is not to be like Willie Mays circa the early 1970's. During the waning days of his career, Mays, one of baseball's all-time great players, could barely perform some of the most rudimentary tasks on the baseball diamond. During Mays' prime, no one was better at tracking down deep fly balls and gliding around the base paths. He performed such acrobatic feats while slugging 660 home runs for the New York/San Francisco Giants. But when Mays struggled mightily at the tail end of his career for the New York Mets, he epitomized an athlete waiting too long to retire.

Upon watching Mays falter during the closing moments of his Hall of Fame career, longtime *New Yorker* scribe Roger Angell scathingly remarked, "his failings are now so cruel to watch that I am relieved when he is not in the lineup."

Angell's brutal honesty was not unwarranted. Mays could barely hit the ball out of the infield and for the life of him couldn't get from first base to third base on a single. For one of the game's most graceful outfielders who could seamlessly flag down line drives soaring over 400 feet, catching a routine pop-up now became a cumbersome task. NBC broadcaster Tony Kubek acknowledged as much to his broadcast partner, the legendary Curt Gowdy, when he said, "Boy, Curt, this is the thing I think all sports fans in all areas hate to see--a great one playing in his last years having this kind of trouble, standing up and falling down." For some baseball fans, it was akin to watching a loved one wither away in senility after a lifetime of sharp intellectualism. It was so obvious to everyone but Mays that it was time to call it quits.

The idea is not to be like Willie Mays, but rather be like John Elway, who won his only two Super Bowl championships in the final two seasons of his career. Jerome Bettis waited his entire career for that elusive Super Bowl ring, which he finally captured in his last game as a pro. David Robinson passed the torch to his successor Tim Duncan but not before he punctuated his storied NBA career with a second world championship in June 2003. But they can't all have a hero's farewell with a confetti dousing no matter how badly they want it to end in that manner.

For others, there are nondescript endings with mildly rewarding sendoffs. Even the greatest of greats feel they have to milk just one more ounce out of their gifted skills. The last time the planet saw its most talented basketball player, Michael Jordan, in a competitive athletic context was during his brief anticlimactic stint with the Washington Wizards. Granted, in the fall of 2001 when Jordan came back to the NBA for the second time, sports were not at the forefront of Americans' collective attention. In the immediate aftermath of 9/11, Jordan's farewell tour in the nation's capital flew under even diehard sports fans' radar screens. Still the reality was that Jordan's second return to the NBA was marked by mediocrity--at least when juxtaposed to his prior dominance.

During the 2002-2003 NBA season, Jordan's last hurrah in pro basketball, he posted 20.0 points per game. It would have been a very impressive total for any other player not named Michael Jordan. For MJ, it was the lowest point per game average by a considerable amount over the course of his historic career. After sinking game winning shots against the Utah Jazz in the NBA Finals and taking over some of the most memorable NBA Finals games against the Phoenix Suns in 1993, Jordan left the game in a rather nondescript fashion. The 2002-2003 Wizards went 37-45 and failed to make the playoffs. It was not an embarrassing finish but rather just a letdown.

He hasn't been the only one to exit that way. When the San Francisco 49ers moved onto Steve Young as their quarterback, Joe

Montana finished his career for the Kansas City Chiefs, a team he led to the 1993 AFC Championship Game. After parting ways with the Dallas Cowboys, Emmitt Smith prolonged his NFL career for two moderately productive seasons with the Arizona Cardinals.

But ultimately, retirement is inevitable, even if some can't admit it. Father Time has an undefeated record in the history of professional sports. Biology dictates slower recovery times and reflexes and thus weaker performances for older competitors. Eventually, the law of diminishing returns sets in the longer one competes against others who are faster, stronger, and younger. With that said, there have been and always will be some who seemingly can't retire from sports.

Ageless Placekickers

When athletes hang around into their mid-forties, team rosters can resemble those in a slow pitch softball league: middle aged guys rub shoulders with kids in their early twenties. Peach fuzz mixes with greybeards. It is understandable that athletic teams, similar to army units, primarily consist of young men who are in the best physical shape of their lives. What comes across as awkward is when men who could be their fathers are occupying nearby lockers.

After recently celebrating his 47th birthday, Morten Andersen, a native of Copenhagen, Denmark, was watching Atlanta Falcons football on FOX during a lazy October afternoon in 2007. He was sitting on his couch drinking a beer while watching one of his former teams struggling to convert field goal attempts. He had a hunch his kicking services might be needed again.

After a Sunday night phone call and Monday night signing, Andersen was back at practice Tuesday morning. That Andersen was easily old enough to be the father of many teammates was not lost on several Falcons. Some were witty enough to place a diagram of a crutch and wheelchair in his locker and kidded that he cried during *Jurassic Park* because it brought back memories for him. Not only was Andersen older than all of his teammates, but he also had seven months on his coach, Bobby Petrino. That is what happens when you spend over a quarter century playing in the NFL.

Morten Andersen's first year was in 1982 for the New Orleans Saints. *E.T.* was the number one movie in America and a gallon of gas cost 91 cents. Morten Andersen's last year was in 2008 for the Atlanta Falcons. While the 2008 recession era gas prices remarkably weren't all that different from those in 1982, it was strikingly obvious that Andersen was playing alongside teammates who were not yet born in 1982.

In 1995, the New Orleans Saints released Andersen, believing he was all washed up. In 2008, he officially retired as a member of the Atlanta Falcons after having been named to seven Pro Bowls. As Andersen played until his late forties, he had to tackle athletic guys half his age on kickoffs. Had Andersen been able to keep his spot on Atlanta's roster past December 6, 2008, he would have been the oldest NFL player ever, breaking George Blanda's record.

During his many years playing, he truly was a Great Dane. Against the heavily favored Minnesota Vikings in the 1998 NFC Championship Game, Andersen kicked the game-winning field goal to seal the Falcons' Super Bowl berth. In a cruel twist of fate, Morten Andersen's winning kick was from the same distance as Minnesota Vikings kicker Gary Anderson's miss moments earlier. Gary was also born in another country (South Africa) and played until he was 45-years-old.

On April 5, 2013, the Detroit Lions parted ways with the retiring Jason Hanson. He had been their kicker for 21 consecutive seasons. His replacement was David Akers, a well-traveled and accomplished kicker who was approaching his forties and showed no signs of retiring anytime soon.

The predicament of placekickers parallels that of slow pitching big leaguers. There is a market for their reliability and grizzled veteran status. For positions that place a premium on precision and accuracy over speed and strength, age does not compromise effectiveness. Changeup artist Jamie Moyer and knuckleballer Tim Wakefield both proved to be effective pitchers well into their forties. At the time of publication of this book, Moyer was in his early fifties and had not officially retired from baseball, acknowledging that he hadn't "closed that door yet."

It's a good deal for both team and player. The team gets a mature employee with a proven track record of productivity and reasonable salary expectations. The player gets to pad career stats, boost his Hall of Fame candidacy, and continue playing sports for a living not long before he hits normal retirement age.

Major League Ducks on the Pond

It would seem like the ultimate paradox: Major Leaguers who pine to go back to playing Minor League level baseball. When you make the big leagues, you want to stay in the big leagues. Almost all of them put in their dues in the Minor Leagues through earning modest salaries and enduring 12-hour bus rides through such remote outposts as Tennessee and Idaho. But it's worth it when you sign your first big league contract and then stay in the big leagues--as long as you never go back.

The problem is that Major League Baseball is no different from any other cold-hearted bottom line business: it's all about "what have you done for me lately." Once superstars are deemed damaged goods, they are not worth paying to keep on the roster. Eerily similar to so many professions, management will give the nod to the younger and cheaper employee.

For most people in working America, they can't wait to try something new when they receive a buyout package or realize it's time to step down. Professional baseball is unique in the sense that some employees will go to great extremes to stay in the same line of work. It is no secret that many players tap into an artificial fountain of youth by taking Performance Enhancing Drugs and Human Growth Hormones. For some players, it is worth the risk of tampering with unethical and illegal practices in order to get quicker reflexes and bounce back from injuries sooner.

If Major League Baseball and their affiliated Minor League teams are no longer interested in a player's services, Independent League Baseball may be a viable option. Whereas many independent teams are stacked with guys who never played past college or the lower levels of the Minors, the Long Island Ducks franchise of the Atlantic League is known as a mecca for former All-Stars who will give anything to return to their days of stardom. While some cynics might dismiss them as washed up stars living in the past, it is hard to not appreciate their genuine love of the game.

The list of Ducks alumni reads like a rundown of late 1900's and early 2000's MLB All-Stars: Rickey Henderson, Juan Gonzalez, Carl Everett, Edgardo Alfonzo, Jose Offerman, Armando Benitez, Vladimir Guerrero, and Dontrelle Willis. Of those players, only Henderson ever actually made it back to the big leagues.

At 31-years-old and still very much in his athletic prime, Willis did not fit the typical profile of an old veteran hoping to recapture some of the magic from his glory days. Willis, also known as the D-Train, was all the rage of Major League Baseball in 2003 when he helped the Florida Marlins capture their second world championship against the New York Yankees. As a 21-year-old rookie, Willis won 14 games and sported a nifty 3.30 ERA. In 2005 Willis was quite possibly the most talented pitcher on the planet when he posted a 22-10 record and 2.63 ERA. Even more impressive was that he did so during a time when steroid usage was still fairly rampant. Major League hitters were trading in their personal trainers for chemists and compiling cartoonish statistics with artificial help. Through stifling so many potent lineups, Willis showed signs of being the best African-American pitcher since Bob Gibson.

Sadly, Willis would tailspin shortly after experiencing early success. From 2008-2012, he won only several games over the course of several pit stops in Detroit, Arizona, and Cincinnati. He took the cliché of falling off the face of the earth to a new level. Unlike many pitchers whose careers are curtailed due to arm ailments, Willis struggled mightily with an anxiety disorder that caused him to be erratic on the mound. When it became apparent that no Major League team was interested in his services, Willis was unemployed.

Like many other athletes, Willis was a young man in his early thirties who had to figure out what to do with the rest of his life after having dedicated his twenties to a profession that had seemed to hit a roadblock. Ultimately, Willis decided that other careers could wait for at least a little while longer. He thought that joining the Long Island Ducks was a last hope for reviving his career and not becoming the rare star athlete to prematurely leave the game due to a non-injury related issue.

"I like playing with the guys and stuff like that. I have played with all these guys before. It's almost like seeing your neighbor when you get to this point. It's a good group and travel's easy. Teammates are good. The one thing I enjoy most is our coaching staff, they're very good. Our pitching coach [Steve Foucault] probably has got 100 years in baseball, he's worked with everybody and he's good about applying himself to each and every one of us as far as the pitching staff. Kevin Baez is the same way. Kevin has been managing in this league for a while and he's played in the Major Leagues. We're a veteran ball club so they kind of just like leave it up to us to get our work in and do the things we've got to do to get ourselves ready to be successful out there. We started off kind of shaky. I think that's one of the things, just playing baseball together and once we got knowing each other and knowing how we play, we've been playing well. That's been fun.

"The travel is easy. I think the farthest we go is Sugarland, Texas but that's flying. Everything's relatively easy with guys working other jobs. It's been fun and guys have been competitive on both sides, especially playing the other teams and guys getting their feet wet being new to the league. With playing guys over and over again it makes it competitive and harder and harder because after a while guys know what guys are going to do against each other."

When the Ducks play across the Long Island Sound in Bridgeport, Connecticut against the rival Bridgeport Bluefish, batters face a backdrop that includes an industrial tower and truckers barreling down I-95 South. Big leaguers enjoy food spreads catered by upscale local restaurants. In the independent leagues, peanut butter and jelly sandwiches are often available for pre-game snacks in the clubhouse. And you play the same teams over and over again, which makes for friendly and intimate competition.

"It's already like these guys from Bridgeport, I have already played against them four or five times. Those guys get 30 At Bats as opposed to the Major Leagues where you might see a team once and you might not see them again for another month or two. But here you might pitch against the team three or four times in a row. It makes for a more competitive ball game."

As a former MLB star who earned tens of millions of dollars, Willis has the financial security that some of his fellow Ducks lack. Even on a team laden with former big leaguers, there are still some guys who never made significant money playing professional baseball. That Willis, a former Rookie of the Year and All-Star, had the humility to play under modest conditions for a team not affiliated with a big league franchise speaks volumes to his perseverance and love of baseball. He embraced playing in Long Island, signing autographs for kids before games and not complaining about staying in motels on road trips. During the waning days of summer 2013, the Los Angeles Angels of Anaheim signed Willis to a Minor League contract. The Angels realized that Willis enjoyed a successful summer with the Ducks and was one step closer to making it back to the Majors. Irrespective of whether or not he would actually return, the D-Train refused to retire from a profession that at times had given him so much joy in life.

In light of the many sluggers and aces who sweat out the drudgery of Independent League Baseball, it is remarkable how some players can take the luxuries of the big leagues for granted. In May 2010, the *Tacoma News Tribune* reported that during the last few days of his career, Ken Griffey Jr. missed a chance to enter a game as a pinch hitter because he was asleep in the clubhouse.

Independent League Baseball is not for everyone. But for some ballplayers who just want to play for the sake of playing, suiting up for the Ducks is a way to postpone retirement. It also shows how life can go from seemingly never ending success to unexpected challenges.

Doing Their Best Satchel Paige Impersonation

In 2012, Roger Clemens showed signs of following in the footsteps of Satchel Paige, a remarkably talented pitcher who appeared in a Major League game when he was 59 years young. In late summer 2012, Clemens briefly pitched for the Sugarland Skeeters. His battery mate was his oldest son, Koby.

"That was a very, very unique experience," explained Gary Gaetti, who was Sugarland's manager at the time. "Roger is a very interesting man not just because of what he was able to do with a baseball but just because of who he is and how successful he was and how popular he was."

Gaetti was on the Houston Astros' coaching staff when Roger pitched for his hometown team and dominated the National League for the first time in his career. The two have remained close throughout the years. As a manager in the Atlantic League, Gary knew teams love creative signings and that there was a natural way to bring Clemens onboard.

"Actually the way it started was I was interested in recruiting his son to play ball. Roger was kind enough to respond to me and in the course of the conversation, I felt like I had the freedom to just go ahead and offer him a contract and say hey this would be a neat thing for the people of Houston and if he was at all interested I could make it possible for him to pitch, even if he just wanted to throw one inning or whatever.

"He never really said why he wanted to come back and pitch but I think it was because he could and he knew he could whether he wanted to prove to any particular person or group of people or the general public or his fans that he could do it. I think at the time there might have been some serious interest in him from some teams making a comeback for somebody that could come in and help someone down the stretch. He never really commented on why he wanted to do it. But he got to do something that has probably never ever been done before--he got to actually pitch to his son who caught the second time he pitched, which very well could have been his motivation. He's got other interests other than baseball too. He has always been a guy that keeps himself in shape so I didn't think the actual physical part of what he did was all that hard for him. It was a really, really special moment. It felt like a playoff atmosphere for us here in Sugarland. It was just a unique experience, something that will probably never be done again--a guy being 50-years-old and getting to pitch in a professional setting to his son."

In his brief stint with Sugarland, the Rocket pitched well, tossing several scoreless innings while still overpowering opposing hitters with his trademark four-seam fastball. After Clemens repeatedly left the game and returned, it appears that the Sugarland cameo is his last time pitching in professional baseball. Strangely, he is not the only former Yankees pitcher to retire and come back on multiple occasions. His best friend, Andy Pettitte, pitched with him in Houston before returning to the Yankees, retiring, and then coming back to the

Bronx. Pettitte is now well into his forties and has finally retired for good. Jamie Moyer, currently 51-years-old and officially still active, is older than his jersey number (50).

* * *

As far as retirement from professional athletics goes, there are all different extremes. The stories of those who seem to play forever get all the attention. But then there is the other extreme of all-world running backs Barry Sanders and Terrell Davis, players who bolted from football when they were at the top of their game. There are certainly others who fall into the Sanders and Davis camp, but for the most part, more leave too late than too soon. The reasons are endless and range from career padding for Hall of Fame candidacy (Harold Baines, Craig Biggio) to being reluctant to give up the luxurious lifestyle. While it seems that many of the pro athletes who hang around into their early forties play finesse positions, hockey stars Jaromir Jagr, Mark Recchi, and Dave Andreychuk played a physically grueling sport well past their 40th birthday. Center Kevin Willis accumulated quite a bit of mileage running up-and-down professional basketball courts from 1984-2007. Those players would seem like cubs compared to Gordie Howe who skated for the Hartford Whalers when he was 51-years-old.

Whether they are objects of abject ridicule or good-natured jokes, guys who notoriously stay in the game well into their forties are associated with their longevity more so than any other characteristic. Had Jamie Moyer retired in the late 1990's or even the late 2000's, he would not be the butt of many jokes. He would just have been considered a very good, if not great, left-handed starter. Others such as Roger Clemens, Michael Jordan, Andy Pettitte, and Morten Andersen seemed to be in a constant state of flux between retirement and work. And then there are athletes such as Manny Ramirez who played in Taiwan as a way to prove he could still compete at a professional level.

One would be hard pressed to find another profession in which employees go to such great lengths to stay with relatively little financial incentive.

EPILOGUE

The public is already well aware of athletes who have stayed involved in their respective sports through becoming successful coaches and broadcasters, so I tried to provide a new perspective on such individuals. Naturally, chapters on sports related careers necessitated copious verbiage. However, I also tried to pay close attention to former athletes who are pursuing non-sports related careers. I felt it would be more interesting to shed light on lesser known tales that illustrate various individuals' interests, some of which flew under the radar screen when they were competing. Hopefully, this book shows that athletes are not just one-dimensional jocks. They can be entertainers, intellectuals, businessmen, attorneys, writers, and community activists. Perhaps, like all of us, they are not immune from boredom during extended periods of idleness and profligacy during short-lived times of great prosperity.

Sports Illustrated's 'Where Are They Now?' issue is an invaluable resource to subscribers as it provides them with a glimpse into the fascinating lives of their childhood heroes. But hopefully this book demonstrates that the current accounts of such individuals warrant more substantial prose than a few terse articles. The accounts chronicled in *Sports Illustrated* represent the tip of an overwhelmingly captivating iceberg. Maybe there is a reason that *Sports Illustrated* chooses to have the 'Where Are They Now?' edition be its only double issue. There is the supply of such stories and the interest on behalf of readers. Perhaps it is no coincidence that the majority of spotlighted individuals in the *Sports Illustrated* issue are actually those who played in the 1960's, 1970's, and 1980's--a time period when salaries (and in some cases egos) were not particularly bloated. A professional athlete was not deemed a full-time vocation. Most had to work other jobs in the offseason, acquiring other skills and interests that could be applicable for non-athletic careers later in life. The modern athlete in one of the four major sports (football, hockey, basketball, baseball) does not have to work in the off-season to be financially comfortable. Overwhelmingly lavish training facilities with state-of-the-art equipment were not rampant throughout Arizona and Florida in the mid-1990's. For modern pro athletes, there has never been a sharper focus on honing their athletic skills and training longer and harder during the off-season to prolong their careers.

As the transition from physical challenges to intellectual ones can be quite an adjustment, it was interesting to realize that most of the athletes who are currently not involved in sports still recognize parallels between their athletic and non-athletic careers. Success in any field, regardless of whether it involves athletics, fame, and wealth, requires an inordinate amount of diligence and perseverance. I still cannot fathom how one can play in the NFL while going to law school at night.

On another level, hopefully this book provided you with a fresh perspective on some aspects of professional athletes' lives. The 24/7 social media blitz often leaves us associating modern day athletes with DUI's, gay slurs, and contract holdouts. The good deeds, insecurities, and literary interests of athletes often evade the public's cognizance.

From a personal standpoint, I started this book at the very beginning of the 2013 calendar year. During frigid January afternoons at Panera, I sat at my computer wondering how I was going to have enough material to provide readers with a fascinating and refreshing perspective on a topic that has received a fair amount of publicity. I soon realized that being alive in 2013 left me with no excuse not to write this book. A good place to start was leaving Microsoft Word for the Google homepage. I got more nuggets of information and interesting leads than I knew what to do with. Never before in the history of humankind has it been so convenient to write a book. Centuries ago, some of the greatest intellectual thinkers to grace the planet would hunch over ink stained paper in a kerosene lit room to craft their timeless masterpieces. Expedient communication consisted of letters arriving in horse-drawn carriages. Now we get frustrated when an email attachment is slow to load. I can't imagine how so many legendary New England authors living in the 1700's and 1800's braved treacherous winters while scripting their literary classics. Working on this book in between sips of hot chocolate during the Blizzard of 2013 was bliss. I was fortunate to embark on a literary project during the right time.

However, during this age of non-stop information, we do have to sift through the clutter of dubious leads to get to gold. I had to be adaptable to follow new leads as they surfaced and then modify the direction of my book accordingly. Some athletes proved more reclusive than J.D. Salinger while others were more than willing to share their stories to an American public that may or may not be losing sight of their accomplishments.

Words cannot express how fortunate I feel to have had this opportunity. I never expected to speak to so many fascinating people in such a narrow timeframe. Working two other jobs and finding sufficient time for research and writing was a juggling act, but it was worth every keystroke, phone call, and email. I hope that others have the opportunity to pursue work that gives them so much joy and pride.

ACKNOWLEDGMENTS

Lists are dangerous as it seems that someone always inevitably gets left out. However, this book would never have been completed if it weren't for the help and support from some very special people who deserve to be mentioned.

Sincere gratitude to the following media relations staff members for taking the time out of their busy schedules to accommodate my requests: Steve East, Heidi Holland, John Blake, Matt Chmura, Dick Kelley, Sergey Kocharov, Amanda Hamman, Michael Polak, Jason Zillo, Paul Herrmann, Tom Felice, Alaina Bendi, MJ Burns, Jonathan Supranowitz, Steve Kirschner, Matt McGuirk, John Kostouros, and Tom Felice. Before my initial email to reach out, I didn't know you and you didn't know me. I am very grateful for your professionalism in helping me arrange interviews whether it was by phone, email or in person.

I can't thank the following individuals enough for spending the time to provide insightful interview responses: Dolph Schayes, Tony Amonte, Scott Young, Corliss Williamson, Shawn McEachern, Ian Kinsler, Joba Chamberlain, Butch Hobson, David Robinson, Steve Finley, Dave Bing, Rich Kelley, Derek Sanderson, Kellen Winslow, Alan Page, A.J. Pierzynski, Warrick Dunn, Mel Owens, Adrian Beltre, Chris Berman, Pedro Gomez, Ron Mix, Dikembe Mutombo, David Murphy, Adam Oates, Rich Kelley, Thomas Ian Nicholas, Bob Melvin, Mark Brunell, Alan Page, Scott Brosius, David Shand, Bob Ryan, Dontrelle Willis, Bill Hall, Ramon Castro, Craig Counsell, Tony Clark, Gary Gaetti, Bobby Valentine, Hubert Davis, Kevin Johnson, and Nicklas Backstrom.

Thank you to Michelle Brown of Mill City Press for serving as my author advocate throughout the entire process. Your guidance and support were beyond helpful.

Evan Grant of the *Dallas Morning News* provided fascinating insight that only someone so well connected to Major League Baseball could offer.

I am very appreciative of Dan Shaughnessy, Aaron Wilson, and Troy Renck for taking the time to endorse my book.

Thank you to my friends, colleagues, and relatives for encouraging me to pursue this project. It was really helpful to have you ask for updates as I was going along.

My in-laws and sister-in law were also extremely attentive to my efforts. They provided invaluable support throughout the writing and researching processes.

I can't thank Mom, Dad, Sharon, and Jonathan enough for their love and thoughtfulness over the past year. They provided some wonderful suggestions that helped me broaden the scope and direction of the book. I am forever grateful for their help and advice throughout the year. I am so lucky to be able to call them my parents, sister, and brother. My dad also took me to my first Red Sox game--before even Mo Vaughn and Butch Hobson were around.

I am blessed and honored to have the greatest wife in the world. From day one, she was endlessly supportive of a project that meant so much to me. I'm pretty sure there is no more astute literary critic alive than Lauren. Her feedback and praise were invaluable assets throughout this year long endeavor. She also knows how to make some delicious dinners for post-writing meals.

Thank you for reading this book. I hope you had as much fun reading it as I had writing it.

BIBLIOGRAPHY

Books:

Goldman, David, *Jewish Sports Stars: Athletic Heroes Past and Present,* Minneapolis: Lerner Publishing Group, 2006.

Hirsch, James, *Willie Mays: The Life, The Legend,* New York: Scribner, 2010.

Kennedy, Kostya, *Hockey Talk,* Plattsburgh, New York: McClelland & Steward Ltd, 2011.

Lewis, Michael. *Moneyball,* New York: W.W. Norton, 2003.

Maraniss, David, *Clemente,* New York: Simon & Schuster, 2006.

McCallum, Jack, *Dream Team,* New York: Ballantine Books, 2012.

McGrane, William, *All Rise,* Chicago: Triumph Books, 2010.

Olney, Buster, *The Last Night of the Yankee Dynasty,* New York: Ecco, 2004.

Sanderson, Derek and Shea, Kevin, *Crossing The Line,* Chicago: Triumph Books LLC, 2012.

Magazine Articles:

Ballard, Chris "If Antoine Walker Shimmies, But It's In Boise, Is He Really Shimmying?", *Sports Illustrated,* March 19, 2012, Volume 116 Issue 12.

Pooley, Eric, "The Art of Being Bill Bradley", *TIME,* October 4, 1999, Volume 154 Issue 14.

Rodriquez, Ken, "The Education of David Robinson", *San Antonio Magazine,* March 2012.

Talbert, Marcia Wade, "Dave Bing Elected Detroit Mayor", *Black Enterprise,* May 6, 2009.

Torre, Pablo, "How (and Why) Athletes Go Broke", *Sports Illustrated,* March 23, 2009, Volume 110 Issue 12.

Wertheim, Jon, "Deepness in Seattle", *Sports Illustrated* July 9, 2012, Volume 117 Issue 2.

Newspaper Articles:

Aldridge, David, "Dave Bing's smooth transition; after NBA, succeeding in big business", *Washington Post,* May 22, 1989.

Brown, Emma, "Drummer Chad Smith and slugger Bernie Williams lobby for music education", *Washington Post,* March 19, 2003.

Buckley, Cara, "Power player", *New York Times,* July 30, 2010.

Holmes, Baxter, "Robert Parish hopes to find work", *Boston Globe,* August 8, 2013.

Madden, Bill, "NY Mets great and Hall of Fame pitcher Tom Seaver feeling better, winning his battle with Lyme disease", *New York Daily News,* March 15, 2013.

Nance, Roscoe, "Mutombo helps Congo take a big step forward with new hospital", *USA Today,* August 14, 2006.

Ostrowsky, David, "Leader of the pack", *Jewish Advocate,* August 4, 2006.

Phelan, Kevin, "Bernie Williams' passion for jazz takes center stage", *USA Today,* June 25, 2013.

Shaughnessy, Dan, "In historically bad taste here", *Boston Globe,* March 11, 2010.

Shaughnessy, Dan, "Shortstop delivered in grand way", *Boston Globe,* June 23, 2004.

Shaughnessy, Dan, "In short, it was time for him to go", *Boston Globe,* August 1, 2004.

Springer, Shira, "No comment no more", *Boston Globe,* August 21, 2011.

Vincent, Roger, "Magic Johnson built business empire after court glories ended", *Los Angeles Times,* March 28, 2012.

Young, Shalise Manza, "NFL coaches doubt staying power of read option", *Boston Globe,* May 19, 2013.

Websites:

Baseball-reference.com

Basketball-reference.com

bleacherreport.com

clintonfoundation.org

Cnnsi.com

Espn.com

Football-reference.com

Greenwellsfamilyfunpark.com

Hockey-reference.com

huffingtonpost.com

kareemabduljabbar.com

Rolandmartinreports.com

voanews.com

Wdc.org/programs/homes-for-the-holidays.html